MATT SMITH
THE BIOGRAPHY

MATT SMITH
THE BIOGRAPHY

EMILY HERBERT

JOHN BLAKE

Published by John Blake Publishing Ltd,
3 Bramber Court, 2 Bramber Road,
London W14 9PB, England

www.johnblakepublishing.co.uk

First published in hardback in 2010

ISBN: 978-1-84358-268-7

British Library Cataloguing-in-Publication Data:

A catalogue record for this book is available from the British Library.

Design by www.envydesign.co.uk

Printed in Great Britain by CPI William Clowes, Beccles, NR34 7TL

1 3 5 7 9 10 8 6 4 2

Papers used by John Blake Publishing are natural, recyclable products made from wood grown in sustainable forests. The manufacturing processes conform to the environmental regulations of the country of origin.

Every attempt has been made to contact the relevant copyright-holders, but some were unobtainable. We would be grateful if the appropriate people could contact us.

CONTENTS

CHAPTER 1
DOCTOR WHO?

The nation had been agog. Just weeks earlier, towards the end of 2008, David Tennant had announced that he was stepping down from his role as possibly the most popular Doctor Who ever, and amid the sadness that he was leaving, there was intensive speculation as to who would take over the role. A new Doctor Who is a little like a new James Bond: an iconic part of Britain's cultural landscape, and whoever gets either part knows that there will be praise and hostility in equal measure. Indeed, so much had David Tennant made the role his own, that it was widely forgotten that when he had originally taken it over from Christopher Eccleston, who in turn had revived the character for the twenty-first century, there had been a fair bit of grumbling there, too.

In the wake of the Tennant decision, however, speculation had reached a boiling point that it hadn't ever done before. The show's canny producers must have been delighted as one name after another was trotted out: would *Cold Feet* star James Nesbitt, often cited in connection with the role, be the next to wield the sonic screwdriver? What about John Simm? The actor, who had starred in the massively popular BBC drama *Life On Mars*, had recently put in a scene-stealing turn as Doctor Who's nemesis The Master, the only other surviving Time Lord: would he now do a leap from the dark side and don the cloak of goodness himself?

There were plenty of other options, too. Paterson Joseph emerged as an early favourite: he had appeared on the show twice already with Christopher Eccleston, and bookmakers Paddy Power were offering odds of 3/1 on him becoming the first black Doctor Who. Another strong possibility appeared to be David Morrissey: he was already known to be appearing in an upcoming episode of the series, and mysteriously appeared to be taking on the role of the Doctor already, even though Tennant had yet to stand down. Then there was Paul McGann, who had actually been the Doctor once already, in a one-off Doctor Who film. Rhys Ifans? Well, he was Welsh and the series was filmed in Cardiff.

Names were flooding in thick and fast. Robert Carlyle and Jason Statham were mentioned. Chiwetel Ejiofor, Anthony Head (already a seasoned monster hunter), David Walliams, Alan Davies, Richard E Grant, Nigel

Harman, Bill Nighy, Richard Coyle, Aidan Gillen, Harry Lloyd and Marc Warren were all in the frame. There was speculation that the next Doctor might be a hereditary one: Sean Pertwee, the son of a previous Doctor Who was mentioned, as were Jack Davenport, Tom Ellis, Adrian Lester (another potential black Doctor), Alexander Armstrong, Daniel Radcliffe, Burn Gorman, Julian Rhind-Tutt, Rupert Penry-Jones, Stephen Fry (really), Ben Miles and even David Suchet. So was Hugh Grant, of all the unlikely people, who was typically self-deprecating: 'The danger with those things is that it's only when you see it on screen that you think, "Damn, that was good – why did I say no?"' he said. 'But then, knowing me, I'd probably make a mess of it.'

Other contenders included Gary Oldman, Paul Bettany, someone called Matt Smith (at odds of 66/1), Benedict Cumberbatch, Dean Lennox Kelly (who had appeared in an episode of *Doctor Who* as Shakespeare), Christopher Villiers, Ricky Gervais and Eddie Izzard. Indeed, everyone who was anyone in the realm of British show business appeared to be being considered for the role.

And that really did include everyone. Russell T Davies, the brilliant screenwriter and producer who had brought the series back to life in 2005, naughtily muddied the waters, when he speculated that for the first time ever, Doctor Who could be a woman. 'Amy Winehouse would be a great doctor,' he said. Come to mention it, why not

Billie Piper, who had also played a big role in the programme's revival as the Doctor's assistant Rose? Or Freema Agyeman, another of the Doctor's assistants, who could go one step better by playing the Doctor as a black woman, yet another first? Or Catherine Tate, another ex-assistant, although certainly not to everyone's taste. Who was it going to be?

Nor was Davies letting it rest there. Aware that his every utterance was going to be pounced on – and rightly so, given what he'd done for the show – he also let it be known that someone quite different was his favourite for the role: Russell Tovey, another seasoned *Doctor Who* performer, who had played the role of Midshipman Frame in the previous year's Christmas special. 'Tovey is my favourite casting of the lot,' he said. 'He's amazing. I think I'd make him the eleventh doctor.' Tovey would certainly not have been averse to signing up. 'Of course!' he said. 'It's awesome!' Somewhat ironically, given who was to get the role, Tovey's youth was seen to count against him – he was only 29.

But it wasn't going to be Russell's decision any more. Tennant wasn't the only one leaving the show: Russell was too, to be replaced by another brilliant screenwriter, Steven Moffat. Moffat had been responsible for some of the most memorable episodes in the recent series, including "Blink", which introduced a brand new and terrifying set of villains, the Weeping Angels, and it was he – and the BBC, of course – who was to determine who was to be the next Doctor. The tension was becoming almost too much to bear.

But neither Moffat nor his colleagues was going to put the nation out of its misery any time soon. Tennant announced he was stepping down in October 2008; the new Who was not to be unveiled until the following January. Meanwhile, the weeping and wailing over Tennant's departure had begun, not least by Tennant himself: 'When Doctor Who returns in 2010 it won't be with me,' he told the BBC in an interview. 'Now don't make me cry. I love this part, and I love this show so much that if I don't take a deep breath and move on now I never will, and you'll be wheeling me out of the Tardis in my bath chair.'

He had been playing it for three years, after all; that was long enough. 'I think it's better to go when there's a chance that people might miss you, rather than to hang around and outstay your welcome,' he said. '[It had been] the most extraordinary time, it's been bewildering, life changing, very exciting. And just so much fun, such a great show to work on. That's one of the reasons I think it's right to take a deep breath and bow out when it's still fun, when it's a novelty. I don't ever want it to feel like a job, so I want to move on when it still feels exciting and fresh and that means I'll miss it.'

He might have felt like that, but not many others did.

David Tennant had been a massively popular Doctor Who and as much as there were vague feelings of goodwill towards his successor, whoever that might turn out to be, people simply didn't want him to step away. Then there was the manner of his departure: just how was Doctor Who going to metamorphose into his next stage? 'I might drop an anvil on his head,' said Davies. 'Or maybe a piano – a radioactive piano.'

As the months passed in the build-up to the big announcement, speculation intensified further still. There were whole internet sites devoted to the question of who would be the next Doctor, with the bookies changing their odds from day to day. At one point Robert Carlyle became the 2/1 favourite (like Tennant, he was thin, lithe and Scottish, although Tennant had always played the Doctor as an Englishman); at another James Nesbitt was garnering odds of 6/1. A Facebook page was established dedicated to getting Zac Efron the role, while Paterson Joseph rose to 3/1.

Discussion boards flourished. Everyone had an opinion, and more than a few of them wanted Tennant to stay. 'I'm going with David Mitchell!!' was one typical online post. 'The Man would totally work, watch some *Peep Show*, *That Mitchell and Webb Look*. Look for more info if you have not heard of him. In fact I second the opinion that Hugh Laurie would make an EXCELLENT doctor, Stephen Fry would also make a very good Doctor and evoke memories of the wonderful Patrick Troughton!'

'It's good to think outside the box,' said another. 'But, obviously, Amy Winehouse would be a terrible choice in basically every respect.'

'I'm cool with Tennant,' added a third. 'I like him a lot, in fact, even though he's a little annoying at times. But I think he's one of the better Doctors. Dunno about his replacement, though. Used to be, they'd sort of pick someone to contrast the previous one, like the bland Davison after the "colourful" Baker (still my fave). But I liked the subsequent choices, too, so whatevs...'

And then there was the odd online heated debate – 'I see no good reason why the Doctor couldn't regenerate in a female form,' snapped one poster, quoting another. 'I didn't say HE couldn't, just that you would have to deal with the whole "male trapped in a female body" thing. If it were done it would be just a cry for attention, unless it were for a short arc, which could be excellent. A body switch between Doctor and Companion could be hilarious for an episode or two.'

Was it any wonder there was so much debate? There always had been, whenever one Who handed over to another, of course, but these days there was so much more because everyone could express their opinions online. And, despite the widespread opinion that David Tennant was the best Doctor of the lot, people still maintained their previous favourites – just as with James Bond, it tended to be whichever actor happened to be the viewer's first Who. Tom Baker certainly resonated with the masses, but all the past Whos had their supporters – which didn't make it any easier to choose who would come next.

Certainly, whoever it was going to be was going to find the role career changing. Most of the earlier Doctors had been at least fairly well known before they stepped into the TARDIS (Time And Relative Dimensions In Space), and although Tom Baker had become pretty much defined by the role, he, like the rest, managed to find a career elsewhere. (Though before Tennant, Baker was consistently the most popular Who, constantly topping polls to that effect and only ever losing three times, once to Sylvester McCoy in 1990 and twice to Tennant in 2006 and 2009).

This time round, although no one knew it yet, the thinking was going to be a little different. The producers wanted a totally unknown quantity, and for that they were going to have to find someone very, very young. That was in stark contrast to the first Doctor, played by William Hartnell, who was the first to play the role at the grand old age of 55; even Tennant, who was 34 when he first went time travelling, had been considered a smidgen too young. Now, however, the producers were on the verge of taking a radical approach by appointing the youngest Who ever – but it was also a massive risk.

'Matt Who?' demanded the headlines. And they were not alone. There was widespread amazement throughout the country, for the BBC had utterly confounded expectations and cast a total unknown in one of the most iconic roles of them all. And not only had no one ever heard of him, but he was so young. At 26, he was the youngest ever Time Lord, three years younger than Peter Davison, who was 29 when he got the part in 1981. Although Matt's name had popped up in the frenzy of speculation that had been gripping the country, no one had taken it seriously – how could you possibly give such a role to someone so unknown and so lacking in years? And however sure they might have been about their new man, the BBC was taking a tremendous risk. That show has to be carried by its central character, no matter how curvy the sidekicks or how threatening the monsters, and for someone who looked to be barely out of his teens, that was an awful lot to ask.

Matt himself was very much aware of what was at stake. 'I haven't slept,' he said in an interview on *Doctor Who Confidential*, of which more later. 'It's an iconic part of our culture … it has the status of Robin Hood or Sherlock Holmes and I'm taking it on. It's nerve-wracking and exciting, I'm flabbergasted. It's a huge legacy [but] I want to be brave enough to make my own choices.' That, if anything, was understating it. Utter incomprehension from everyone else ruled the day.

Gareth McLean, writing in the *Guardian*, summed up what Matt could, if he pulled it off, expect – and the dangers it entailed. 'You can understand actors' reticence about taking on the role,' he wrote. 'Tennant has been such a definitive doctor that there will be those who have forgotten all about Christopher Eccleston. Further, the commitment required – the gruelling filming schedule and the ardent Who fans that one must court or at the very least tolerate – coupled with the intense tabloid scrutiny that playing the Doctor inevitably attracts aren't exactly incentives for taking on the role. Then again, playing the Doctor has catapulted Tennant into British TV drama's A-list. Similar things can be said of a post-Rose Billie Piper, and even a guest appearance in *Doctor Who* can work wonders for an actor's career.'

The comments that accompanied this were mixed: 'This is an awful bit of casting' ... 'This is a piece of stunt casting to make the show stupidly trendy and popular with 13-year olds' ... 'I got a good feeling instantly from him' ... 'As a fan of the first Doctor Who all those years ago who enjoyed Eccleston but struggled with the appalling concept of Doctor-in-Luv I shall now give up' ... 'Having a leader of the Tory party younger than me was traumatic enough. I don't see how this lad can have any authority with an older, established character' ... and so it went on. It was never going to be a smooth handover whoever was chosen, simply because David Tennant had been so incredibly popular – but an awful lot of people were expressing an awful lot of doubt.

There was also a certain amount of disappointment that after all that palaver, Doctor Who was indeed going to be yet another white man. 'The idea of a black or woman Doctor is something we only seem to be able to enjoy as a tease,' said Matthew Sweet, the cultural commentator and long term *Doctor Who* fan, sounding a little rueful. 'When Tom Baker left, for example, there was speculation about Joanna Lumley taking over. There is a little part of me that's disappointed the Obama effect hasn't reached Gallifrey yet. [But] This was one of the best-kept secrets. Matt Smith has got a fascinating face. It's long and bony, with a commanding jaw. He looks like someone who could have been in Duran Duran. He has a quality of the old man trapped in the young man's body. I suspect he might be a more sensual character than David Tennant, who had no kind of dangerous sexuality about him. There's something Byronic about Matt Smith – he's got the lips for it.'

His appearance was certainly one indication that the BBC might just have got it right. Matt is a slightly unusual looking man, with a slight resemblance to the slim and cheek-boned David Tennant, but with an otherworldly air about him that gives him the appearance as someone with origins in outer space. It is important that Doctor Who should have an air of the outsider about him, as well – not just because he's an alien, but because he's the last of his species. The Doctor has seen civilisations destroyed, peoples forever vanquished. He must be able to emote melancholy. Matt Smith, it seemed, might just be able to do that.

All the BBC big guns were standing up for their man, as you would expect them to, of course, but that also helped. 'With two hearts, a ferocious mind and over 900 years of experience behind him, it's not every 26-year-old actor who can take on the role like the Doctor, but within moments of meeting Matt he showed the skill and imagination needed to create a Doctor all of his own,' said Piers Wenger, head of drama at BBC Wales.

David Tennant, crucially, was also extremely supportive: 'As I begin the end of my connection to all of this, I do feel a bit of jealousy of Matt who's just about to start and has got all of this ahead of him. It's a very exciting journey to go on,' he said.

Of course, a whole industry had grown up around the phenomenon that was *Doctor Who*. There were people taking an educated interest in what was going on across the board: people who followed the interests of the characters, the series and the fans. These were the people who reflected what the man on the street was thinking, and once the shock had begun to subside, the public was coming round to the idea that this might just turn out to be an inspired piece of casting after all.

As was only to be expected, a heated debate began on the web. Any number of science-fiction forums joined in, each eager to have their say, starting with SciFi.com (now Syfy.com):

'Interesting choice, though not someone I'm familiar with ... I'll have to find something he's been in. I'm sure that won't be his costume because it's a leather jacket away from being a carbon copy of Eccleston's, and I suspect that they'll save the reveal of the costume for another press roll-out.' – The Oncoming Storm.

'An interesting choice. His face and hair reminds me of a Pertwee/Tom mixture and he seems eccentric enough in real life so ... here's hoping all the best for Matt in 2010.' – Tardispoo.

'May your Tardis run smooth, your sonic occasionally fail you, your companion NOT fall in love with you, the Daleks not bother you and may your run be glorious!' – LibrarianEmie.

'Steven Moffat himself has said he was convinced the actor needed to be in his late 30s or early 40s but was blown away by Matt, so that gives me great confidence. So congrats to Matt and looking forward to seeing him in series 5!' – Astoreri.

And from Kasterborous online magazine:

'I knew I'd feel some trepidation whoever was cast ... and I do. I suspect this chap is a fine actor and hopefully will be able to carry on where the excellent

Tennant left off. My main worry is that they may have given themselves a problem with casting other roles. Will all companions have to be 25 or under?' – mcnessa. (This was an early contribution to the next topic of heated debate, namely the identity of the Doctor's next companion.)

'He is suitably a bit weird looking, energetic and physical so hopefully he will ditch the rather maudlin air the last two Doctors had and redefine the Doctor rather than just being a continuation of the "Hooray trouble, solved it but now I'm a bit lonely and depressed" character that the Doctor has become of late.' – Dr Hula Hoop.

And from The Guild fan site, the following:

'Well, I hope his personality lives up to the hype. Supposedly he "wow'd" Moffat.' – Chris F.

'This kid looks very, very, very young. And in my head, anyone called The Doctor should look at least old enough to be a doctor. That is my biggest problem. So, what? The next doctor will be the kid from *The Sarah Jane Adventures*?' – Jeff Carlisle.

'I know nothing about this guy. I honestly wish they had picked someone a bit different looking. He doesn't look like a Time Lord to me. Seems too young looking/preppy.' – Danubus38.

'I'd seen David Tennant in *Casanova* and liked him in that, but Matt Smith didn't make a huge impression on me in *Ruby in the Smoke*. I didn't catch *Party People*, maybe that was better.' – Grr Aargh.

'I've only seen him in one thing, too, so I don't know what to expect. I'm surprised. I didn't want to like David when he took over but he won me over. Hopefully Matt will, too.' – Raven Kai.

Then there were the sites dedicated to *Doctor Who* alone – a fair number due to the huge popularity the series had managed to maintain. These were the sites the fans flocked to and it was important they were onside – as indeed, most were. 'We think it is a great choice to have someone so young. David Tennant was the most energetic Doctor ever, and you need somebody with youth and energy to take that forward,' said Sebastian Brook, editor of the Doctor Who Online fan website.

He was not alone. A programme called *Doctor Who Confidential* had been running on BBC3 for some years. Usually it was an accompaniment to the actual series, and featured interviews with cast and crew members to get their take on the episode that had just been shown. Now, however, there was a one-off special to discuss the appointment of the new Doctor Who.

It gave the fans their first chance to get a really good look at the new Doctor. Matt Smith had appeared in a few previous productions, which were now being dug up and reviewed, but he was such an unknown quantity that this was the first time many people got a chance to see what he was really about. He certainly had a certain otherworldly quality about him: slim to the point of gauntness, his hair teased into an extravagant quiff, while a dark jacket over a dark sweater betokened the style that was to come.

Matt certainly struck the right note. There was no preening, swaggering, 'Look at me' behaviour on display – if anything, he seemed staggered by the honour that had come his way. 'It's like an iconic part of our culture,' he said. 'My granddad knows about it, my dad knows about it – it's been going since 1963. It's my responsibility. It's exciting. Nerve-wracking. Exciting. It stops you sleeping.'

Matt also described what his initial reaction was when he'd heard he got the role. 'I paced around the room for about three days,' he said. 'I didn't know what to do so I'd get up and come back and I'd sit down and I'd watch a bit of TV. And then I'd smile and go, "I'm the Doctor." It does weird things to you.'

Of course, it was made all the more difficult by the fact that Matt could not rush outside and yell his brilliant news to the rooftops. The announcement had been shrouded in total secrecy until the BBC had been ready to reveal who their next man was to be; Matt was not able, therefore, to share with very many people or indeed to calm the media speculation that was reaching fever pitch. 'It was a complete nightmare not being able to tell anyone about it, because like any secret, it bubbles up inside you and the longer you keep it, the more mad you go, I think,' he revealed. 'And the more you're trying to suppress it. And then, I'll be in my flat, watching the TV and *Doctor Who* will be on and my flat mate's there, and I'd be watching it thinking, "I'd love to share that I'm the new Doctor. But I can't." It was also quite exciting, as it gave me a sense of mischief – I know something that the rest of Britain doesn't know. Privy to cool information, as it were.'

Anyone watching the interview should have been be pretty sure by that stage that *Doctor Who* fans were in safe hands. Matt was in turn charming, self-deprecating and, without overdoing it, humble about the legacy that had been entrusted to him. He was clearly taking it every bit as seriously as the fans would expect, while at the same time relishing the opportunity that had come his way. And who wouldn't? For all the burden of expectation that was resting on his shoulders, one way or another, Matt's life was never going to be the same again.

So did he really manage to resist the temptation to tell anyone? 'I had to tell someone, I was going mad. So I told my dad,' said Matt. 'Because I just had to tell someone. But it's like a giant secret that is hugely significant. He was rather flabbergasted. He sort of laughed, really. And he was very proud, because he loves the show. And then he started talking about Tom Baker, and his references, and that's the thing. My whole family have references for it. And when my granddad found out, I didn't know what he was going to do with it. He was just immensely proud and excited. And what do you do with information like that? It's such a – "I'm going to be playing the Doctor!" Even now when I say it, it freaks me out – in a good way. He was excited, proud, elated.'

Matt's father Dave was pretty overwhelmed by it all, too. 'When he called, he said, "Dad, just call me the Doctor." And I said, "What, are you not well?"' Dave later recalled. 'Then I realised and just started jumping around, it was surreal really. There were a couple of nights when my wife Lynne and I just sat up and talked about it, because we couldn't talk about it to anybody else.'

Of course, the competition had been intense. Matt had been up against half the theatrical establishment of Britain, or so it had seemed at times – so just what, when it boiled down to it, had the actual audition been like? 'I don't know, I just tried to do my best,' said Matt. 'I tried to give my version. And be brave with it and make brave choices. It was very surreal, though, because again, I couldn't tell anyone about it. It was a bizarre process. I've never had an audition like it, really.'

So what did he actually have to do? 'I had quite a lot of scenes to learn, and I got the scenes the night before,' said Matt. 'So I had sort of four or five scenes to learn and there were too many lines to learn the lines the night before, so I just had to learn my way around the scenes as much as I could. And we practised the scenes, as it were. And I get some notes and we'd have a talk about it – I wish I could tell you what's in the scenes. It's fun; there was a lot of stuff going on.'

All of this was happening, of course, before filming had actually begun. But Matt did have some idea of what was on the cards. 'I've read episode one and episode four – I'm not supposed to say that,' he said, clasping his mouth in alarm, looking for all the world like a naughty schoolboy. 'And they rocket along. He's a brilliant writer, Steven Moffat. Even a funny writer. I can't say a lot about them, but you're in for a treat.'

And what of his actual interpretation of the role? Just what kind of a Doctor was Steven's Doctor going to be? 'I've got this wonderful journey in front of me, where I've got six months to build this, this, Time Lord,' he said, beaming. 'That's such an exciting prospect, because I love that part of being an actor. I love the discovery of it and the being a detective bit. That excites me hugely. But I don't know – I've got to build him up.'

There was another aspect to it all, as well – the attention he was going to get. All the other actors in the role had experienced enough success to put them in the public eye before they actually stepped into the Tardis. But Matt hadn't. How on earth was he going to deal with that? 'I have been warned about what to expect, and I think David's going to be quite a good source of information as well,' he said. 'Because he's dealt with it with great grace and dignity and enthusiasm, and that's what it's about. And I think you work so hard as the Doctor on *Doctor Who* anyway, you don't really get time to be in the public eye. I don't know. I've talked to a couple of people about it but I'm just going to concentrate on the words on the page. Let the rest unfold.'

The programme was an extremely charming introduction to the new man, but if Matt really thought he wasn't going to be in the public eye, he could dream on. Given the speculation there had been before his appointment and the degree of controversy it aroused afterwards, there was absolutely no way Matt wasn't going to find himself at the centre of attention for some time to come. The debate continued to rage on the Syfy.com website – although judging from that, the producers had pretty much got it right. 'I was a bit worried when they said he was the youngest ever, but I'm really pleasantly surprised,' posted a Mr Bryn. 'As [Steven] Moffat says, he's young but he also looks old at the same time.'

Calibanz agreed. 'I get the feeling that this casting is going to prove the right choice,' he said. 'I was hoping for a relative unknown without a fixed public image and the Moff has gone for that.'

But not everyone was pleased. Another forum joining in the debate was Kasterborous online magazine, as quoted above: one contributor, Funcho, wasn't a happy bunny at all. 'Too young! *High School Musical* in space!'

Oldskool138 felt the same: 'The Doc's supposed to have a commanding presence (even McCoy's Doc had presence). This guy looks like he slouches into a room rather than one who's trying to solve a problem and help people out. I'm not a huge fan of the question-mark vest or Technicolor nightmare coat, but can we have the Doctor dress a little more eccentric rather than like he just walked out of a boutique. His clothes should be more Salvation Army than Rodeo Drive. And the dude's too young. There, I said it and I'd say it again if I had to. Peter Davison was young but not as young as this guy. To me, it looks a bit like stunt casting. They have the old fans watching the show and their young kids but they don't really have that 18–28 demographic.'

Another demographic taking an active interest in all that was going on was the population of Wales. Both David Tennant (a Scot) and Matt Smith played the character as English, but the rejuvenator of the show, Russell T Davies, was Welsh, and so Wales felt it had a special say. And the action was filmed in Cardiff, which stood in for London: hardly surprising, then, that the people of Wales felt they had a special relationship with the show.

Martin Hackett, a historian from Trewern, near Welshpool, was a very long-standing fan, having followed the series since the 1960s. He, too, was a little cautious about Matt Smith's age in taking on the role, but was adamant that he should be given a chance. 'Tennant has such charisma and had established himself in Casanova before striking a rapport as the Doctor, so it will be difficult for anyone to follow him,' he said. 'A lot of names were mooted for the role, including Vic Reeves and Graham Norton, because it would take a big personality to carry off the role. I was expecting someone established like Don Warrington who played Philip in *Rising Damp*. It will be hard to judge Smith until we see him.'

A much younger fan, the type the producers seemed to be reaching out to, was also a little perturbed. 'It was quite a shock when I saw him and I was dubious,' said Owen Jones, 18, from Cardiff. 'But after hearing his eagerness and enthusiasm for the role he seemed to fit it,' he said. 'They have gone for a unique doctor who will bring flair to the role.' Despite being in the target age range, incidentally, it was noticeable that one of Owen's reservations was that he was only eight years younger than the new hero of the show. Even youngsters, it seemed, appeared to think that a 900-year-old Doctor needed to carry some gravitas.

As it happens, Matt was going to succeed quite brilliantly in making the role his own. But it was all very different from the very first Doctor – decades and decades before.

CHAPTER 2
THE DAWN OF
A LEGEND

The year was 1963. The top brass at the BBC had a problem: there was a vacant slot between *Grandstand* and *Juke Box Jury* on Saturday night, and something was needed to fill it. But what? Perhaps, someone ventured, a science-fiction series? Something that might amuse the viewers for a show or two before they came up with something a little more permanent?

As it happened, the idea of a science fiction show had been on the minds of the bosses at Auntie for some time. As far back as March 1962, Eric Maschwitz, the assistant and adviser to the controller of programmes at BBC Television, had asked Donald Wilson, the head of the script department, to have a look at the possibility of producing a science-fiction show; an initial report by Alice Frick and Donald Bull of the BBC Survey Group met with a very positive reaction from Wilson, Maschwitz and Donald Baverstock, the BBC's assistant controller of programmes, the following month. A further report was commissioned by Alice Frick and John Braybon: this time round, they suggested a series based on the idea of time travel. This received a very positive response, although the form of the Doctor himself had yet to appear.

In December that year, nearly 12 months before the first ever *Doctor Who* went out, matters took a another step forwards. Sydney Newman was appointed head of drama at BBC Television. Newman, originally from Canada, and a seminal figure in British broadcasting in the 1950s and 60s, was a big fan of science fiction, commissioning several series in his native country before moving to the UK. There could scarcely have been a better person to take the idea to. And so, work on the programme began.

Initially, a series of meetings were held to discuss the idea with all the BBC staff writers who had prepared the two reports, along with another writer, CE 'Bunny' Webber. Donald Wilson and Bunny Webber were deeply involved in the planning and started to draw up a list of potential characters; it was Newman, however, who came up with the two critical elements that would make the show. The first was the idea of a space/time machine that was bigger on the inside than it was on the outside, and the second was the character of the Doctor himself. It was also Newman who came up with the title: *Doctor Who*.

A team began to assemble. A producer was appointed, Verity Lambert, who was to become another BBC legend. David Whitaker signed as the story editor, while Mervyn Pinfield was brought on board as associate producer. He was also there to provide back-up support to Lambert, who was seen to be lacking in experience at the time. Webber prepared a draft of the first episode, which was written up by the Australian Anthony Coburn, who was also the man who suggested the time machine resemble a police box. And so the Tardis was born.

At the time of writing, *Doctor Who* is the longest running television science fiction series anywhere in the world, and it is almost certainly the calibre of the people who were initially involved that made it so. You could not call it a coincidence that so many people who were to become major figures at the BBC were in at the beginning, but it was certainly a happy combination of circumstances. Back then, however, no one had a clue that what they were working on was going to end up as one of the most famous television shows in the world. Indeed, its initial format was actually totally different from how it ended up, because *Doctor Who* was actually initially conceived as an educational series rather than a piece of straightforward entertainment, with the Tardis assuming a different appearance each week. One week it would be a column in ancient Rome, the next an Egyptian sarcophagus and so on, until someone realised just how much all of this would cost. The idea was hastily dropped; instead, the Tardis's 'chameleon circuit' was said to be malfunctioning – hence its long-term appearance as a police box.

There remained two crucial elements to put in place: the show's theme tune, and the actor who would play the character of the Doctor himself. The first of these was the result of a collaboration between Ron Grainer and Delia Derbyshire; again, resulting in a tune that is almost as iconic as the series it went on to create. Grainer wrote the score in collaboration with the BBC Radiophonic Workshop, while Derbyshire used a series of tape recorders to record sounds made with both concrete sources and square- and sine-wave oscillators, electronic circuits that can be used to produce sound. She then joined the sounds together to such extraordinary effect that Grainer asked, 'Did I write that?' when he first heard it. He had. The title sequence, with the police box hurtling through space, was also put together now, designed by the graphics designer Bernard Lodge and created by Norman Taylor, an electronic effects specialist.

And so all they needed now was a Doctor, something that was easier said than done. Although no one involved had particular long-term hopes for the show, it was still important to get it right, and so a series of actors were approached with a view to taking on the part. Hugh David (who later worked as a director on the programme) and Geoffrey Bayldon had both been approached and both had turned down the role when another name came up – William Hartnell. Nearly 30 years older than Matt Smith was when he stepped into the iconic shoes, Hartnell was a fairly well-known and respected 55-year-old character actor. Hartnell had, in fact, become worried that he was being typecast as a stern army type as he had been playing a number of such roles, although it was his performance in something very different, *This Sporting Life*, that brought him to Verity Lambert's attention. Hartnell wasn't too sure at first – a television series about an alien with no name who travels the galaxy in a police box? – but after a while he said yes. It was probably the best decision of his entire career.

Hartnell, the only child of a single mother (he never discovered the identity of his father), was born in St Pancras, London on 8 January 1908, and died on 23 April 1975. He was to play the role for three years. Although he did go on to take other parts after his stint as Doctor Who came to an end, that is the role for which he will always be remembered and which, for a brief period, he made his own.

The first ever episode of *Doctor Who* was an episode called 'An Unearthly Child', but because of various problems in the course of its production, it had to be re-filmed. (Strangely enough, the same thing happened to the first episode of *Star Trek*.) This gap between the two versions produced a number of important changes. For a start, the Doctor gained a kindlier temperament than his original, grouchy character. There were also changes to costumes and special effects. But as far back as that, all the elements that have maintained the series were there: the sonic screwdriver, the near magical powers which were to get the doctor out of many a sticky scrape and, of course, his companion.

'The Unearthly Child' is, in fact, a reference to that companion, Susan Foreman, played by the actress Carole Ann Ford. Susan was a 15-year-old schoolgirl (at least the assistants have always been very young), but after some unease on the part of the producers at the idea of a young girl travelling alone with a late middle-aged man, it was decided that Susan would be the Doctor's granddaughter. This went on to produce some conundrums that the series has never entirely resolved. If Susan was his granddaughter, then presumably the Doctor must have had a child – and, indeed a spouse – somewhere along the line, but in every subsequent series the Doctor is seen as utterly alone, the last of his race. When David Tennant became the Doctor, he managed to produce a child in a slightly different way from the conventional one (a machine produced her – long story) and there were also heavy hints that the character played by Alex Kingston was once, or would one day become, his wife – but the Doctor has not ever really been portrayed as a married man. In the 1990s, there was some suggestion that Susan was not his natural granddaughter, but that was not the situation posited at the time.

And so the story kicked off. The Doctor and Susan (presumably also a Gallifreyan) are living in London, where they settled to make repairs to the Tardis; Susan takes the name Foreman from a junkyard near where they live. Like her esteemed grandparent, Susan appears to have talents that rather set her apart from her fellow schoolchildren, so much so that her schoolteachers Ian Chesterton (William Russell) and Barbara Wright (Jacqueline Hill) have their suspicions aroused. To find out what is really going on, they follow Susan back to the junkyard where she is living in the Tardis with her grandfather. After hearing her voice in a police box, they enter and find themselves in a very different place from the one they thought they had seen from the outside. And so they, too, became companions, establishing the tradition of a main Doctor's assistant and a couple of extra voyagers, again a tradition that exists to this day.

The very first episode of *Doctor Who*, when it was broadcast, received just about no notice at all. The timing couldn't have been worse: it went out at 5.15pm, on 23 November 1963, a difficult day to debut any television series, given that President John F Kennedy had been assassinated the day before. And if that were not enough, there was a power failure in some parts of the country and those few people who might actually have been interested in watching wouldn't have been able to do so. Indeed, the situation was so dire that the following week the BBC actually repeated the first episode before showing the next.

Nice ploy; shame no one was really interested. The Doctor described himself and Susan as 'wanderers in the fourth dimension', but they might have been wandering into oblivion for all that the majority of television viewers cared. These days, when a show must become a hit instantly or not at all, *Doctor Who* might not even have been re-commissioned, but Verity Lambert and co. knew they had a gem on their hands, and were determined to make it work. And so in the second series, appeared the final ingredient in the mix; the one that made the nation sit up and take notice. It was the introduction of the Daleks.

However, that almost never happened as well. Terry Nation, a scriptwriter, and Raymond Cusick, a designer, came up with the idea of the Daleks. The characters' back-story went through several changes, but the original idea was that they had been a species called the Dals. After a war with the Thals, they mutated into hideous and malevolent beings, which resided inside powerful, individual travel machines; both the casing and the inner mutant has changed in the course of the series, but the basic prototype was laid down here. Daleks, as someone once memorably put it, could be said to resemble giant salt-and-pepper shakers with an arm that resembles a sink plunger; their powers, however, were terrible to behold. They have a single mechanical rotating eye, an exterminator arm containing a death ray, and a 'sink plunger' that can do anything from crushing a man's skull to measuring his intelligence. In short, they are not creatures to be messed with. In their earliest incarnation they appeared to glide an inch or so off the ground, their traction provided by a large, omni-directional rotating device; later on it was stated they move by psychokinetic power. In 1988, by courtesy of the hover power they adopted, they also learned to climb stairs.

Back in 1964, however, they were utterly unintelligible, and given that the series had had a very shaky start indeed, seemed a very unnecessary risk. It is not putting it too strongly, however, to say that this particular battle of the Daleks was the element that made Verity Lambert's name. Donald Wilson, her boss, was very anti the idea of putting them on screen and advised her to drop Nation's script. Verity, however, insisted that they would have to go with it, not least because there was nothing else they could use. And so the Daleks were born.

The series in question had several titles throughout its production stages but came to be best known, quite simply, as *The Daleks*. The Doctor and his travelling trio land the Tardis in a petrified jungle, and after some debate and a little deception (the Doctor pretends the

Tardis is out of mercury), manages to persuade his travelling companions to explore the futuristic city just visible on the horizon. Once there, Barbara is separated from the rest of them – and at the end of the first episode, there is the first ever sighting of a Dalek. Or rather, at the cliffhanging end of the first episode, a long metal arm attached to a being that is as yet unseen.

In the second episode, Susan is sent back to the Tardis to fetch anti-radiation drugs, where she meets the Thals, who are at war with the Daleks. Despite the Doctor's avowed intent to avoid violence, the time travellers are finally forced to advocate just that: initially, Susan attempts to broker peace between the two races, and believes she has succeeded. However, the Daleks double cross her and attack the Thals when they are supposed to be exchanging food. The Doctor, his companions and the Thals manage to escape and get back to the Tardis, where the Thals, avowed pacifists, are taught by the travellers not to give peace a chance. They attack the Daleks and believe they have wiped them out – although, of course, that proves to be completely wrong.

Doctor Who Kremlinologists, of whom there are a fair few, might be interested in the following: this is the only time the Daleks depended on static electricity from the floor of the city to move. It is also made clear that the Daleks require radiation to survive; again, the only time this appears to be the case. The fourth episode of the story is the one in which the Daleks' incredibly famous catchphrase is used. The Doctor and his friends have managed to escape via a lift. 'Make no attempt to catch them, they are to be exterminated, you understand, exterminated,' one Dalek proclaims. 'Exterminate...' – it was to become one of the most fearsome commands of them all.

The series caused a sensation. Whereas the first *Doctor Who* had been largely ignored, now the public couldn't get enough of it. All the elements came together – the police box that was a vast space machine inside, the Time Lord cast apart from the rest of his species (except for his granddaughter, of course, the source of future continuity problems), a few more hangers-on, and fearsome monsters the likes of which television had never seen before – this was the breakthrough the show's producers needed. *Doctor Who* was now very firmly established in the public eye. Donald Wilson, he who had initially been so Dalek-averse, was a big enough man to admit that he'd made a mistake: it was said that he told Verity he wasn't going to try to overrule her again. She clearly knew what worked.

And the Doctor's character itself was able to evolve. Although he was always on the side of good, the earliest incarnations of the Doctor were also very grouchy, and they evolved into something much warmer before the public noticed what was taking place on their television screens. He even occasionally displayed signs of ruthlessness (as, indeed, he did during the very last stages of his incarnation as David Tennant – or, at least, a slight problem in the ego department), and this was largely gone by the time the public had noticed who he was. The Doctor was able to evolve, both as a performance and in the mind of his creators, before he had the pressure of mass audiences. With the Daleks' popularity, viewing figures were to be upwards of 12 million, making it a massive success.

Even so, it was not plain sailing. In 1965, plainly destined for greater things, Verity left to become one of the all-time greats at the BBC. She was replaced by John Wiles who, by all accounts, did not get on very well with William Hartnell (later it was to become apparent that Hartnell was in the early stages of the arteriosclerosis that would claim his life, a decade later). At the time, however, it merely appeared that Hartnell was having problems learning his lines. Various writers left and by 1966 it was apparent that William would be forced to do the same. His ill health was becoming increasingly apparent; though by this time a hugely popular figure, he just couldn't cope with the demands of the role any more.

This presented the makers of the programme with a problem. *Doctor Who* had become a hugely popular series and though the lead actor was about to depart, there was a strong feeling within the BBC itself that there was a good deal of leeway for the series to carry on. It seemed simple: replace him with another actor. John Wiles, the new producer, and Donald Tosh, a screenwriter, set about actioning this plan: they wrote a story called 'The Celestial Toymaker', the idea being that the Doctor would be invisible for a part of the show, and when he reappeared, it would be as another actor.

The new head of serials, Gerald Savory, however, point blank vetoed this idea, with the result that Wiles and Tosh both left the show. That didn't solve the problem, though. By now William Hartnell's health was such that it was obvious he was going to have to leave and when Savory, too, moved on, the producers of the show finally got their chance.

Wiles had been replaced by Innes Lloyd and it was he, in conjunction with the story editor Gerry Davis, who worked out a plan. They were going to have to bring in another actor, there was no doubt about that – but previously, the idea had been to bring in someone else to play the same role. Now they began to toy with the idea of making it the same Doctor – but with a totally different character and personality as well as a different appearance. Why not? He was an alien being. He didn't have to subscribe to the rules that the rest of us did.

And so began another part of the *Doctor Who* legend. Initially it was to be called a process of 'renewal'; in the future, of course, it became a process known as 'regeneration'. And so the Doctor regenerated – this time into the actor Patrick Troughton. Troughton appeared at the end of an episode called 'The Tenth Planet', which also introduced another of the iconic villains the Doctor would have to face – the Cybermen.

Like his predecessor, Troughton, who was born in London on 25 March 1920 and died on 28 March 1987, was a competent character actor, who was also to become best known for playing the part of Doctor Who. Like Hartnell he spent three years in the role, and the two had even acted together, in a film called *Escape* in 1948. He also had a distinguished career in theatre, but from the mid 1950s onwards preferred to work in television. Doctor Who was not his first iconic role (in point of fact, it wasn't even iconic back then), that honour going to Robin Hood, and he was a well-known face on telly by the time he stepped into the Tardis. But that is the role he is most certainly remembered for now.

Just as David Tennant voiced approval about the appointment of Matt Smith, so William Hartnell gave his blessing to Patrick Troughton, saying, 'There's only one man in England who can take over and that's Patrick Troughton.' Troughton was to prove a popular figure with fellow cast members and crew, and played the role quite differently – as a 'cosmic hobo' à la Charlie Chaplin, an approach suggested by Sydney Newman.

Indeed, there was now a comic dimension to the role

that hadn't existed before, although this Doctor, too, had a dark side, occasionally manipulating the truth when it suited his ends. The Cybermen were proving very popular and the Daleks made a welcome return (however many times they were to be wiped out, somehow the producers always found a way for them to make a comeback), but it was a very heavy workload – 40 to 44 episodes per year. (Due to the BBC's policy of wiping tapes in order to save money, not many of those episodes still exist.) That workload, combined with a fear of being typecast, finally got to Troughton, and in 1969, he, too, prepared to step down.

As has happened time and again in the history of *Doctor Who*, the programme, like its central character, needed to regenerate, and now proved to be just such a time. Viewing figures were beginning to fall (indeed, there is talk, hotly denied in some quarters, that the show was threatened with the axe even as far back as that); in addition, time travel was proving extortionately expensive – for the BBC, that is. Every time the Doctor landed somewhere new and exotic, it required vast amounts of props and costumes and they simply couldn't afford to keep on spending at that rate. And so great minds began thinking about what the step would be.

Various ideas came up. The first was that the Doctor's travels should be confined to earth, and this premise was briefly put forward in an episode called 'The Invasion', in which the Doctor was captured by his fellow Time Lords (like the Daleks, the extinct Time Lords also had a habit of reappearing when the producers got stuck) and sentenced to exile on earth for the crime of interfering with other races. There was talk that he should act as Scientific Advisor to the United Nations Intelligence Taskforce, or UNIT for short. Troughton duly took part in that episode, but while it proved popular with the public, a Time Lord who couldn't travel through time and space was a Time Lord short of adventures. And so the idea was dropped – although it had been enough to save *Doctor Who* from the chop.

The advent of the third Doctor was going to usher in some other changes, too. For a start, until now, *Doctor Who* had been filmed in black and white: now and from then on, the show moved into glorious Technicolor. Then there was the new Doctor. The producers had approached Ron Moody, then best known for playing Fagin in *Oliver!*, but he wasn't interested, and so the role ended up going to Jon Pertwee. Pertwee, like the two Doctors before him (this was becoming a noticeable trend) had had plenty of experience elsewhere, primarily as a comic actor, but it was for this now increasingly iconic role that he was to be best known.

John Devon Roland Pertwee was born in London on 7 July 1919 and died on 20 May 1996. From a rather distinguished background (the family was descended from

Huguenots and his full surname, un-anglicised, would have been de Perthuis de Laillevault), Jon attended RADA (Royal Academy of Dramatic Art) and was an officer in the Royal Navy, working in naval intelligence during World War II. With a faint resemblance to Danny Kaye, which was exploited in full in the film *Murder at the Windmill*, Jon began to make his name as a comic actor, mainly courtesy of two radio shows, *Waterlogged Spa* and *Puffney Post Office*, alongside a very longstanding role as Chief Petty Officer Pertwee on *The Navy Lark*, which ran from 1959 to 1977. He also appeared in some of the *Carry On* films, displaying a lightness of touch that many assumed he would bring to the part of Doctor Who.

But he did not. Jon Pertwee was a very popular Third Doctor, and outlasted both his predecessors in the role in that he stayed for four years, but Jon, the first Doctor of the 1970s, played the role totally straight. In fact, he became something of an action Who, riding motorcycles, hovercraft, the Whomobile and a vintage roadster nicknamed Bessie; he also was soon to resume his travels in time and space.

Until now, *Doctor Who* had been shown up to 44 times a year, a staggering workload for everyone involved. Wisely, this was scaled back, and from the seventh season in 1970, Pertwee's first, the runs were much shorter. That one was 25 episodes and from then on, they were to veer between 20 and 28. Another piece of *Doctor Who* mythology fell into place at this time: in the eighth season, they introduced another villain, The Master. But The Master was no ordinary villain: conceived as Professor Moriarty to the Doctor's Sherlock Holmes, The Master is another Time Lord. But he is an evil creature, the Doctor's mortal enemy, and he recurs up to the present day. His first appearance was in 'Terror of the Autons' in 1971, played by Roger Delgado, who stayed in the role until he was killed in a motorcycle accident in 1973. The identity of the actor playing The Master garnered a great deal of attention in its own right: he has been portrayed by Peter Pratt, Geoffrey Beevers, Anthony Ainley, Eric Roberts and more latterly, Derek Jacobi and John Simm. As a Time Lord he, too, could regenerate, which was convenient when it came time for an actor swap.

Delgado's death shook Jon Pertwee badly, and was one of the factors in making him decide to leave the show. Katy Manning, who'd played his companion, was also moving on, as were various people employed in the production side, and Pertwee was said to have felt it was time to go. And so entered the Fourth Doctor, still considered by many to this day to be the greatest of the lot. He is also, to date, the actor to play the role for the longest time, serving for a full seven years.

When Tom Baker was chosen for the role, many in the audience were shocked. He was much younger than his predecessors – a mere 40 – and was a hard-living, bohemian character off-screen, much married (at one point to Lalla Ward, who played his assistant) – and hanging out with the Soho crowd. Thomas Stewart Baker was born on 20 January 1934 in Liverpool; like all the others he came to be defined by the role. But he stood out head and shoulders above the rest, until David Tennant finally started to beat him in the popularity stakes. But even now, there are very many fans that think he was the best.

When Tom Baker took on the role of *Doctor Who*, his professional life wasn't going at all well: unable to find acting jobs, he was working on a construction site, which led to the nickname 'Boiler Suit Tom'. That didn't last long, though: in his long coat and even longer scarf (which came about by accident when costume designer James Acheson gave too much wool to the knitter, Begonia Pope – Baker himself suggested he wear the finished result), Tom became quite the nattiest Who to date. His Doctor also had a great fondness for jelly babies (a taste shared with Ronald Reagan) and he quite simply made the role his own. Plotlines became darker and scarier, leading to a complaint from Mary Whitehouse, chairwoman of the National Viewers' and Listeners' Association, that young viewers might be traumatised, but viewing figures soared higher than ever. In time, they were forced to lighten up a bit, with Baker adlibbing very successfully, finally gaining up to 19 million viewers for some episodes of the series *City of Death*.

Tom Baker was an incredibly hard act to follow, and despite some sterling performances, no one ever quite did. Peter Davison, fresh from the success of *All Creatures Great and Small* was a natty Fifth Doctor, and probably the best looking (and, at 29, youngest) to date; he was followed by Colin Baker as the Sixth Doctor, Sylvester McCoy as the Seventh, Paul McGann, in a TV movie, as the Eighth – and that, would have appeared to be that. By the end of the 1980s, *Doctor Who* appeared to have run out of steam. In 1989, Jonathan Powell, then Controller of BBC1, suspended the show, and although the BBC said it would one day return, no one really believed him. It had had an incredibly good run, but they'd been there and done everything that they possibly could. *Doctor Who*, it seemed, was no more.

But one man had a very different take on it all. An increasingly successful player on British prime-time television throughout the 1990s, one man thought that not only was there still a lot of mileage left in *Doctor Who*, but that it could scale greater heights than ever before. That man was Russell T Davies – and he was about to bring about one of the most spectacular comebacks television had ever known.

CHAPTER 3

DOCTOR WHO REGENERATES

'All planets have a North' – the Ninth Doctor

Doctor Who had lain dormant for over a decade. The younger generation vaguely knew the programme as something their parents had watched; the parents had fond memories. But it was over. It was a programme that had had its day. Shaky sets, iffy special effects and a certain dated quality attached itself to the name – *Doctor Who* was a very happily remembered but lost part of the nation's past.

But one man didn't think like this. He believed that *Doctor Who* had a huge role to play in the twenty-first century, that the franchise was not dead but sleeping, and that, in short, it was high time *Doctor Who* made a comeback. And this particular man was in a position to do something about it.

Stephen Russell Davies was born 27 April 1963, in

Sketty, a suburb of Swansea, and he was to make his beloved homeland a very crucial part of the series he was shortly to revive. Russell went to Olchfa School and, like most children of his generation, he adored watching *Doctor Who* on a Saturday night; he went on to read English Literature at Worcester College, Oxford. After that he attended a Theatre Studies course run by Cardiff University and based at the Sherman Theatre, before joining the BBC. He took the in-house director's course, as a prelude to a career behind the cameras, and around this time, in the late 1980s, added a T to his name to distinguish himself from a well-known radio presenter. Russell T Davies was on his way.

Although it was a series for adults that was to make his name, Russell really learned his trade in children's television, something that a decade or so later was going to stand him in very good stead. He was part of the children's department at BBC Manchester from 1988 to 1992, producing *Why Don't You?* and beginning to write for the first time. He wrote three episodes of the children's comedy series *ChuckleVision* and he also created *Breakfast Serials.* In all, this was perfect training for the seismic effect he was going to create when the Doctor finally reappeared in 2005.

Russell's first venture into science fiction came in 1991, when he wrote a six-part children's drama called *Dark Season*, a very successful venture starring the young Kate

Winslet. This was followed by *Century Falls*, another children's serial, although this time with a very much darker edge. In 1992, he moved to Granada Television, where he produced and wrote the children's drama series *Children's Ward*. In 1996 a sign of what was to come emerged, when Russell was introduced to Virgin Publishing and ended up writing a *Doctor Who* novel, *Damaged Goods*. More successes followed, as he began to move towards adult television, contributing to *Coronation Street*, among many others, and becoming a full-time writer on period drama *The Grand*. Within the world of television, it was this that really made his name.

But it was another series that was to introduce him to the wider world. Russell left Granada to join another organisation, Red Production Company, where he worked on a programme called *Queer As Folk*, first broadcast on Channel 4 early 1999. The series charted the lives of three gay men living in Manchester's gay village around Canal Street, Stuart (Aidan Gillen), Vince (Craig Kelly) and Nathan (Charlie Hunnam). The series was for more explicit about homosexuality in both its subject matter and dialogue than mainstream audiences were used to, eliciting a certain amount of shock. But it brought Russell to the attention of the wider populace.

Even then, however, as he was busy shocking the grown-ups, there were signs that Russell had something else on his mind. Put simply, *Queer As Folk* was littered with references to *Doctor Who*. There was the episode where Vince was given a model of the Doctor's robotic dog, K-9. A copy of *Damaged Goods*, that *Doctor Who* novel, was left in Vince's bedroom. On another occasion, Vince and a conquest end up watching *Genesis of the Daleks* and on a further occasion still, Vince has to choose between two men, Cameron and Stuart. He goes for Stuart, because Stuart could name all the actors who have played Doctor Who.

If that wasn't an indication of what Russell was thinking, nothing was. He continued to work on television programming for adults, winning Writer of the Year in 2001 at the British Comedy Awards, and in 2003 he worked on TV serial *The Second Coming*. This won him a Royal Television Society Award. It also got him acquainted with the programme's star – Christopher Eccleston.

Unlike most writers and producers, Russell was now a famous man in his own right. But despite the groundbreaking nature of *Queer As Folk*, it was not to be until the mid-Noughties that Russell could be said to change the face of television, with the reintroduction of *Doctor Who*. Russell had made no secret of the fact that he was a fan of the series: in particular he cited Robert Holmes, who was a writer in the Tom Baker days, saying that he had written some of the best dialogue ever to be heard on television. He had also said that the only thing that would tempt him back to the BBC would be the chance to work on *Doctor Who*.

As far back as 1999 that possibility had, in fact, been on the cards. Russell had held meetings with the then BBC1 Controller, Peter Salmon, which had ultimately come to nothing. One of the problems was that BBC Worldwide wanted to make another *Doctor Who* film. However, nothing had come of that either, and by 2003, BBC1, now being run by Lorraine Heggessey, again decided to stake a claim to the famous name. Along with the BBC's Head of Drama Jane Tranter, Lorraine approached Russell. One of the biggest upheavals in recent television history was about to begin.

On 26 September 2003, it was announced that Russell T Davies was going to become the executive producer and chief writer of a new series of *Doctor Who*, the first to be filmed in more than 15 years. Filming would take place in Cardiff and the new show would air in 2005.

'It's funny because, as a long-term fan of the show, it was like I was a 40-year-old focus group, working on what worked and what didn't,' Russell said, shortly before he stepped down. 'I never liked the Time Lords. I always thought they were slightly boring and bumped the programme down, so the decision to get rid of them was just immediate.' In actual fact, of course, they too were to reappear.

Russell was very aware of what a unique programme it was and the hugely different ways in which he could take it further. 'It's such an unusual show because it's different every week,' he said. 'You can do a comedy episode. You can do a dark, psychological episode. You can have romps. You can have love stories. Because it's always changing, you don't need to worry too much about the change. We all just hang on for the ride, really.'

The usual speculation began about who would be the new Doctor, especially important now as it would to all intents and purposes involve totally recreating a character most children were now unfamiliar with: on 20 March 2004, it was announced that the Ninth Doctor was to be Christopher Eccleston.

Born 16 February 1964, Christopher, unlike Matt, was neither extremely young nor unknown when he took on the part. Born into a working-class family in Salford, Lancashire, Eccleston (like Matt) originally wanted to be a footballer, but found that his real talents lay in acting. He did two years on the Performance Foundation Course at Salford Tech, before moving to London's Central School of Speech and Drama. His career took off slowly, but he began to make his mark.

In 1991, Christopher had his first real breakthrough, when he won the part of Derek Bentley in the film *Let Him Have It*, after which repeated appearances on *Cracker* began to register him in the public's eye. In 1994 he took a step up further with a role in *Shallow Grave* (Ewan McGregor was a co-star); two years after that, he started in the very successful *Our Friends In The North* (Daniel Craig was a co-star). He was well and truly on his way.

As usual, however, *Doctor Who* was to overshadow everything before and since. From the moment Christopher hit the screens in 2005, a very cool Who, complete with northern accent, to inform his assistant Rose Tyler (Billie Piper – possibly the most famous assistant to date) that, 'Every planet has a north,' the role was his own. But for reasons that were never entirely clear, Christopher was only going to take on the role for one season. Some people believed he feared typecasting (and indeed, he is one of the few Whos to have escaped that so far) and others that he found the workload too burdensome, although that was later hotly denied. Either way, or for whatever reason, he wasn't going to stay in the role for long.

And he certainly appeared to be happy enough at first. What was it, Christopher was once asked, that attracted him to the role? 'The scripts, which are mainly written by a writer called Russell T Davies, whom I've worked with before,' he said. 'The character was very different from anything I'd done before because he's very funny and light, and I've done a lot of heavy, serious drama. Actors are only as good as the script they're speaking – and these are good scripts.'

He had also actively sought out the role himself. 'I emailed Russell T Davies and I asked him to put me on the list of people he was going to audition,' said Christopher. 'And then I auditioned and they taped it, and I got the role.'

Unlike everyone else involved in the new venture, however, Christopher had not been a long-term fan. It was perhaps this that made him realise the dangers of staying in the Tardis for too long – although he was to become very shirty when asked about it after he departed the role. For him, it appeared to be the new challenge rather than nostalgia that appealed.

'I wasn't a huge fan of the series but there are two things I did tune in for,' Christopher said. 'Firstly, the regenerations – when one actor took over the role of the Doctor from another actor. I thought it was fascinating that it was the same character but he looked different, and I wanted to see how they did it special effects-wise. And secondly, to see the inside of a Dalek. The Daleks are the Doctor's greatest enemy and they are brutal and sinister and vicious but they also have something else going on inside them. There were always a couple of episodes where that would be revealed. And that was fascinating – the psychology and the special effects. We have that in the new series.'

Christopher was tactful enough not to be drawn on the issue of past favourites. 'No that would be wrong to say,' he said. 'The Doctors in my time were Patrick Troughton, who was the first one that I saw and in a way I lean towards him because he was the first one I saw. I thought Jon Pertwee was fantastic and Tom Baker I also thought was fantastic.'

Then there was the new assistant. Billie Piper was also a curious choice: until then she had been best known for a brief pop career and an equally brief marriage to Chris Evans. She was to prove a spectacular success, and unlike Christopher, would stay for more than one series. However, at the time she was very much an unknown quantity.

'They love each other,' Eccleston said of the relationship between the Doctor and Rose. 'They're best friends and they kind of finish off each other's sentences, understand each other's mood swings and reasoning but, as in all good relationships, they have lessons to teach other. Traditionally over the last 40 years, the Doctor has been the hero and the companion is a bit vulnerable. But here we've got an equal – we've got a hero and a heroine. She saves his life later in the series. She's as brave and courageous and intelligent as he is.'

No *Doctor Who* would be complete without the monsters, of course, and there were going to be plenty in the new series to send children behind the sofa. 'In episode eight, there are creatures called the Reapers – they terrify me,' said Christopher (and if they frightened

Doctor Who, what chance the rest of us?). 'The Slitheen are pretty frightening and there are the Gelth, and Cassandra from episode two. But for me, it would be the Reapers. They fly and they plunge down from above. They're allowed on to planet earth because there's been a break in time. It's like a wound in the natural order of things and they slip through. And the Daleks – they're frightening. Not in the way they look – as they look quite old-fashioned – but the psychology is very frightening. They're the Doctor's Achilles' heel and they know all about his history, and they are able to understand the way his mind works. So it's the psychology of Daleks as much as anything – apart from the fact they want to take over the world!'

Christopher was hopeful this would all have the desired effect on the viewers. '[It will] terrify them, I hope!' he said. 'And move them and entertain them. The Doctor's really concerned that people accept other life forms, regardless of colour or creed. If he's got a problem, he will always think of some curious way to approach it. He just loves life – hopefully it will encourage children to love life.'

The series, when it first aired, garnered very positive reviews. Christopher was generally agreed to be a grittier Doctor, Billie was a revelation, and while there was some grumbling from diehard fanatics about changes to the theme tune and title sequence, it was generally judged to be a huge success. There was widespread astonishment, then, when four days after the series debuted on 26 March 2005, the BBC released a statement from Eccleston saying that he was leaving after one series, because he didn't want to be typecast.

Confusion deepened when it then emerged that the statement went out without Christopher's consent. Later in the year, Christopher was asked what it was like to work on the show: 'Mixed, but that's a long story,' he replied. Nor was he very pleased when the actor Alan Davies said that Eccleston had been 'overworked', something he point blank denied. There was some degree of anger from fans about the decision, so much so that the website Outpost Gallifrey (now Gallifrey One) actually had to close down for two days as postings became so heated. It was certainly a shock.

It has never been made entirely clear exactly what lay behind it all, although the closest anyone came to finding out was when Russell T Davis gave a speech at the National Theatre. He addressed the subject head on, saying that Christopher's contract had been for a single year because no one had known whether the revived show was going to succeed. But succeed it did. Eccleston turned out to be a hugely popular Doctor, and won the Most Popular Actor at the National Television Awards for his portrayal of the part.

Whatever his subsequent feelings about the show,

Christopher was enormously touched by the reaction he got from the fans. 'In all the 20 years I've been acting, I've never enjoyed a response so much as the one I've had from children and I'm carrying that in my heart for ever,' he said. But the fact remained – he was off. And in his place there would shortly step the person many believe to be the greatest Doctor of them all.

David John McDonald was born on 18 April 1971 in Bathgate, West Lothian, Scotland, and grew up in Ralston, Renfrewshire, where his father, the Reverend Alexander McDonald, was the local Church of Scotland minister. David was the youngest of three: he attended Ralston Primary and Paisley Grammar School, where he started taking part in school productions, partly encouraged by his English language teacher Moira Robertson. From very early on, it was obvious that David had a real talent.

David was three years old when he told his parents that *Doctor Who* had inspired him to want to become an actor. Fourteen years later, he began to pursue that goal in earnest when, aged 17, he became one of the youngest students at the Royal Scottish Academy of Music and Drama. In the intervening years he became obsessed with *Doctor Who*, watching every episode he could and even meeting the great Tom Baker at a book-signing event in Glasgow. He had a Tom Baker Doctor Who doll, and would allow his obsession to impinge on his schoolwork – for example, by writing an essay on Intergalactic Overdose.

When the time came to join Equity, the actors' union, there was already a David McDonald on the books, and so, taking his new surname from Neil Tennant of the Pet Shop Boys, David Tennant was born. David's professional debut came about when he was still 16 and at school: he took part in an anti-smoking film made by the Glasgow Health Board. His career took off rapidly, with many performances with the Royal Shakespeare Company, as well as on television – and in 1996 he appeared in the film *Jude*, in which he shared a scene with Christopher Eccleston. Many other performances followed, including the lead in *Casanova*, and the part of Barty Crouch Jnr in *Harry Potter and the Goblet of Fire*.

When the news first broke that *Doctor Who* was to return to the screen, David's name came up in connection with it, although he eventually lost out to Christopher Eccleston. When Eccleston stepped down, however, the role went straight to David – although he was not to become the first 'kilted Doctor'. Instead, he employed an English accent for the role.

As with his predecessor, David was drawn by the quality of what was on offer. Yes, he had always been a huge fan, but that was not the only reason he wanted the role. 'I responded to what was in the script,' he said. 'I tried not to sit down and work out a list of self-conscious quirks because I think it can become cloyingly quirky, in the wrong way. I think idiosyncrasies are better born than imposed, so I just responded to what Russell had written. We just bumbled through it, really.'

One early indication of the rapturous response his Doctor was to provoke was when he was greeted with mild hysteria at Comic-Con (a comic book and popular arts convention in San Diego). 'It was great fun,' he said rather proudly. 'It was such an extraordinary experience. I wanted to crowd dive, but they were all sitting down. It was a bit disappointing for me. I figured that was probably the only opportunity in my life that I was going to get to do that. I should have done it.'

Christopher had denied that he was much of a *Who* fan when growing up; David, on the other hand, could scarcely believe his luck. 'Who wouldn't want to be the Doctor? I've even got my own Tardis!' he proclaimed. The first viewing of the Tenth Doctor came towards the end of 2005, when he regenerated at the end of 'The Parting Of The Ways'; his first full outing was the Christmas 2005 special, 'The Christmas Invasion'.

There had been widespread disappointment when Christopher announced that he was stepping down, but the new boy soon proved to be something else. The chemistry between the Doctor and Rose was terrific and the monsters were getting scarier with each episode. His immersion in the role was complete: he didn't just play Doctor Who on television, but also voiced the role for an animated version, read audiobooks, appeared with Peter Davison in a *Doctor Who* special for Children In Need and ended up being voted for as the 'coolest character' on UK television. He had fulfilled his childhood dreams and then some – and the nation was absolutely lapping it up.

The Tenth Doctor went through a number of assistants. Rose had fallen in love with him and so Russell T Davies allowed her happy ending: another, human, version of the Doctor was created and the two of them went off to live in a parallel dimension. The Doctor's second assistant was Martha Jones (Freema Agyeman); she had the hots for him, too. (So, by this time, did quite a number of the fans.) Kylie Minogue appeared in an episode called 'Voyage of the Damned' as a waitress called Astrid; another assistant was Donna Noble (Catherine Tate).

'Everyone said I would adore working with David, and they were right,' said Kylie afterwards. 'He made me feel at ease. I also felt he trusted me, which was important – it was a step back into acting for me. My time on *Doctor Who* was hard work, but I felt somehow I was "home".'

Russell was well aware of the importance of the assistants. 'That's been a vital part of the format,' he said. 'You've got a man who's 906 years old, and he's an alien, and he's a Time Lord. He's wonderfully human, but he has that huge other dimension of being practically immortal and hugely wise, which is dangerous. The human person just brings him down to earth, literally. In the old days of the series, the companion wasn't quite so well developed, but that wasn't the purpose then. Now, in bringing it back, to have the female lead attract people, not just Billie Piper but of Catherine Tate status, to the series, you've got to write it well, otherwise you're not going to get them. One of the joys of the whole show was to work with people like that.'

As David's Doctor just got more and more popular, he found himself having to cope with a level of fame that he wouldn't have been able to imagine before. Perhaps it was his enthusiasm for the role; perhaps it was just because he was so very good at it, but fans just could not leave him alone. David was mobbed everywhere he went; there was intense interest in his personal life, and this merely intensified when it emerged he was going out with Georgia Moffett, who not only played his daughter (sort of) in one episode, but was the real life daughter of the Fifth Doctor, Peter Davison. 'You know you're going to have to cope with it on some level, but until it happens to you I defy anyone to really know what it feels like,' he said. 'When I saw people who were famous, and people whispered and pointed, it felt as though a very powerful individual had walked by. And actually, once you are that person, it just feels scary. All the time.'

The presence of Billie Piper helped. 'She'd been

through it for years,' said David. 'And she had it much worse – women tend to. She had become such a great friend and a real help through the madness that was beginning to explode. And then losing her, and thinking: "I'm on my own!"'

David was perhaps the first of the Doctors to become an out-and-out heart throb, a 'Timephwoard' as one person put it. Billie certainly noticed his appeal.

'I resisted jumping his bones,' she said rather inelegantly, 'but women really fancy him. He's got a gorgeous face, and an energy that's contagious – the spirit of a child. My girlfriends were all in love with him. He's avoided any scandal because he keeps shtoom. He very rarely talks about anything that isn't related to his career or acting. You never see him falling out of clubs. He's never off his face. He's got far more patience than I have. I don't mind signing autographs, but it becomes the topic of conversation at every social event you go to. It starts off: "So how are you?"' Then it's: "Anyway, about *Doctor Who*..." It's at that point I start reaching for the wine.'

But no one was a keener Who fan than David: he had been one all his life. The fact that he and the fans all loved the character was another element to it all: *Doctor Who* meant as much to him as it did to them. There was no way he was going to mess it up. And the stories just got better and the bad guys (or monsters) scarier. John Simm was brought in as the latest incarnation of The Master and he, too, garnered enormous praise.

But all good things must come to an end, and that applied to David Tennant's Doctor, too. Acutely aware of that typecasting issue, and very wisely realising that it was better to leave at a time of his own choosing, rather than being forced out, after four years in the role, David decided it was time to step down. Russell was thinking about moving on, too. It had been quite a ride for the two of them, and Russell, in particular, could claim to have changed the face of Saturday night television, creating a drama that all the family were interested in. But it was time to move on.

The two could be forgiven, however, for waxing a little nostalgic, as they looked back over the show. Russell adored the Daleks, thinking them the greatest villains ever. 'Yes,' he said. 'Better than anything. Better than Darth Vader. Better than Satan. My greatest joy is them working again, after all these years. Everyone said we should redesign them, and it's the one thing I dug my heels in on. That felt like madness at the time.'

And then there was the issue of time travel itself. 'Who wants to see what happened in the past?' he enquired (although Tennant's Doctor had certainly gone backwards as well as forwards). 'I know what happened! The one thing I'll never know is what happens in the future. That drives me mad, it really does

– in 10,000 years, what will this planet be? It's terrible not to know.'

Given the quality of the writing and the production, it was hardly surprising that David's departure was probably both the most dramatic, and the most touching, to date. For a start, the Doctor appeared to be developing a Messiah complex. In an episode entitled 'The Waters of Mars' (which appropriately featured terrifying monsters, zombie-like creatures with faces like cracked mud, who gushed copious amounts of water), the Doctor, *sans* assistant, lands on Mars on what he realises is to be the final day of a Mars mission manned by Adelaide Brooke (Lindsay Duncan), which for unexplained reasons, self destructs. It had been drummed into the head of the Doctor and the viewers that he must not interfere in the course of human history (and those zombies are a clue as to why the mission blew itself up), but the Doctor starts to feel omnipotent and saves them. Adelaide, when she realises what he's done, shoots herself anyway.

The last episode of all, 'The End of Time, Part Two', managed to be a tearjerker on top of everything else. The Doctor knows he is about to die: the prophecy, 'He will knock four times' looms (although no one knew quite how that was going to happen). David Tennant was in no doubt about the effect it was going to have on the viewers – he was already sad enough.

'Coming to the final episodes, you think will these live

up to one's hopes for what that finale will be?' he said on BBC *Breakfast*. 'And then you read the script – the Doctor's been told he's going to die, he knows he's going to die, so you get to play that new flavour with this character that you've got to know so well ... suddenly you're playing a man who knows his end is coming. He's been told: "He will knock four times", and you get The Master with these four beats in his head and you think, well, that's what that is. When you find out tomorrow night what that really means – [it] just breaks your heart – it's brilliant.'

But it wasn't The Master, who had by now been revealed as having been driven mad at the age of eight, when he looked into the Untempered Schism and saw the entire vortex; ever since he had heard four drum beats – the 'drums of war' – in his head. It was someone totally different. The Doctor manages to escape all manner of The Master's unpleasantness only to see that his sometime companion Wilfred Mott, Donna Noble's grandfather, quite brilliantly played by Bernard Cribbins, is trapped in a chamber and will be exposed to radiation unless the Doctor sacrifices himself. To attract the Doctor's attention, he knocks – four times. The end is nigh.

The Doctor duly sacrifices himself and is allowed a quick tour of duty around many other cast members, times and places, before it's time to meet his fate. Ood Sigma, one of the race of telepathic humanoids known as the Ood, appears to tell him that the universe will sing him to sleep: 'This song is ending, but the story never ends,' he says. The Doctor prepares himself and mouths his last words, the last words of what had been one of the most popular characters ever to be seen on British television. 'I don't want to go,' he says.

CHAPTER 4
GERONIMO!

To say that Matt Smith had a hard act to follow was much like commenting that the Atlantic Ocean was a little wet. It didn't even begin to sum up what was required of him: not since the glory days of the great Tom Baker had a Doctor been quite as popular, and even then, when Peter Davison took over, the pressure then wasn't what it was now. For a start, there was no internet, no fan sites, no instant messaging and no reaction from the rest of the world to deal with as soon as it hit the screen. If Matt were to pull it off, he would have to hit the ground running – and then some.

After his brief appearance in the two-part special 'The End Of Time', Matt made his debut proper in the first episode of the latest series, 'The Eleventh Hour'. In the final stages of his previous incarnation, the Doctor had sent the Tardis, but the energy surrounding his regeneration is such that it goes crashing back to earth, where it finally settles in the back garden of a young girl called Amy Pond. There is some slapstick humour between the two of them as the Doctor tries out every type of food he can find in the kitchen in an effort to establish his new tastes, before the real story line begins. Amy leads him upstairs to investigate a crack in her bedroom wall, a crack that the viewer will learn is actually a crack in the very fabric of the universe, and one that will return over and again as the Doctor's adventures with Amy begin.

Forced to attend to the Tardis, the Doctor promises that he will be back in five minutes; in actual fact, he overshoots somewhat and returns 12 years later. Amy is now a young woman, wearing the uniform of a policewoman (in fact, she's a kissogram) and the usual crisis surrounding the continuation of the earth's very existence soon begins. That crack in the wall had allowed Prisoner Zero to escape from a race called the Atraxi, who now want him back: if he doesn't appear, the earth will be incinerated. The Doctor eventually ensures Prisoner Zero is returned to the Atraxi. The earth has been saved, yet again – for now.

The story, which was written by Steven Moffat and had some typically Moffat-esque moments – Prisoner Zero hiding in a room that is usually invisible in the house (it can only been seen out of the corner of your eye) was setting the stage for what was to come. Viewers met the new companion, Amy, of whom more anon, and her boyfriend Rory, who was also set to travel through time and space. It laid out the new Doctor's style: manic, running everywhere and with brilliant comic timing.

Every Doctor has a unique appearance and Matt stood out here, too. Initially he is seen in the battered remains of the Tenth Doctor's last outfit, leading Amy to refer to him as the 'raggedy Doctor'; however, towards the end of the show, he began donning the outfits that would become his.

He raided the local hospital's changing room (explaining this away by pointing out that he had just saved the earth for 'the millionth time') and procured a rather donnish outfit consisting of a brown tweed jacket with elbow patches, rolled up trousers, black boots and a bow tie. One frequent refrain throughout the show is that, 'Bow ties are cool.' There was grumbling in some quarters about this, with some fans saying it was an outfit better suited to an older man, but Matt was tall and slim and could carry it off. And it was certainly better than the original planned alternative: the journalist Benjamin Cook, a great Doctor Who aficionado, described it as 'a little like something Captain Jack Sparrow wears in the *Pirates of the Caribbean* movies.' But Matt demurred at the suggestion, saying that it wasn't the kind of thing the Doctor himself would choose to wear. Rather, Matt wanted to hark back to the style of the Second Doctor, as played by Patrick Troughton, whom he had adored when he first saw him in 'The Tomb Of The Cybermen'.

The series began on 3 April 2010, and met with a broadly positive response. 'The moment the Tardis crash lands in an English country garden … Smith faces down any doubters with aplomb. Smith might turn out to be one of the best Time Lords of the lot,' said Sinclair McKay, in the *Mail on Sunday*. Benji Wilson, in the *Daily Telegraph*, wrote, 'It was ridiculous but it felt right: mad, alien, brand new but very old. A+ to the casting director. A+ to Smith.'

Matthew Bell, in the *Observer*, said: 'From the moment he appeared, dangling from the doorway of his time machine, the new boy demonstrated that he can more than fill the shoes of his predecessor. Matt Smith fights aliens. He wears tweed. He loves custard. He is the Doctor. And he might be more the Doctor than anyone who was the Doctor before.' And Roland White for *The Times* wrote: 'The previous doctor, David Tennant, smouldered his way across the space-time continuum. Smith is more of a geek-chic Time Lord … Smith is a much more quixotic, light-hearted Doctor than Tennant, who seemed to carry the cares of the universe on his shoulders.'

And so the Doctor, Amy and occasionally Rory, began to explore the universe. Their first port of call was to

Starship UK, in an adventure called 'The Beast Below', which had an exceedingly green theme. The entire population of the UK had been put on a colony spaceship, which is ruled by a woman called Liz 10 (also a member of the Royal family, and the starship's queen). The Doctor quickly realises that there's something a little odd about this starship, in that it doesn't appear to have an engine. Even in the engine room, the controls turn out to be false.

Meanwhile, Amy is already displaying all the independence that a modern Doctor's assistant is expected to have. She accompanies a little girl called Mandy, who has lost her brother to 'the beast below' because he wouldn't follow the advice of the sinister 'Smilers', who resemble fairground machines and who guard the ship. Amy discovers a hole covered by a tent that appears to contain a tentacle; she hastily withdraws and finds herself in the hands of the Winders, who take her to a voting booth. Every five years, the residents of the ship are called upon to vote. There she witnesses a video that tells her the truth about the ship: she is offered the choice to protest the result or to forget. Like everyone else, she chooses the latter route.

The Doctor arrives and chooses the protest option, which plunges him and Amy into the bowels of the ship. There they discover the truth. The ship indeed has no engine, rather it is being supported on the back of a giant star whale, who had come to earth to help the fleeing population at the time of the solar flares. Humanity, however, promptly captured the whale, and had been guiding it by blasting electricity into its brain, brutally torturing the poor animal. Liz 10 is revealed as Queen Elizabeth X, who ordered this act centuries previously; every 10 years, she has her memory wiped so she will forget what she has done. The same happens after her subjects have been allowed to vote – although they are always given a choice.

The Doctor, distraught, prepares to render the poor whale brain-dead, which will at least put it out of its pain. However, at this point Mandy's missing brother turns up – because the whale will not harm a child. Amy takes the initiative, and presses the 'abdicate' button, thus freeing the whale – which to the surprise of everyone starts to move faster, given that its intentions were entirely benign in the first place. Amy makes a comparison between the whale and the Doctor: both showed up to save the human race.

The episode, which managed to be touching, innovative and terribly exciting, was well within the *Doctor Who* pantheon. The solar flares, which had caused earth to be abandoned, took place in the twenty-ninth century and had previously been referred to in 'The Ark In Space' and 'The Sontaran Experiment'. Liz 10 refers to the fact that the Doctor has met many other British monarchs, which he has indeed, including Victoria and Elizabeths I and II.

Audiences loved it and so did the critics. In *The Times*, Andrew Billen awarded it a full five stars. '*Doctor Who* ... showed what quality writing was like in Matt Smith's second outing in the title role,' he wrote. 'Saturday's The Beast Below sparkled with ideas and wit while providing nightmarish images – in the form of arcade machine ventriloquist dummies – to keep the kiddies sleepless. Older viewers will have spotted the tribute to Terry Pratchett in the giant whale that powered a space station version of England across the universe. Older ones still will have appreciated the topicality of an election in which citizens every five years "choose to forget what they have learned". Sophie Okonedo, no less, was a splendid future Queen Liz, and Karen Gillan came into her own as the Doctor's deceptively wise companion, Amy Pond.'

Keith Watson, writing in *Metro*, felt the same. 'Sparks there are aplenty in *Doctor Who* (BBC1) as Karen Gillan's winning turn as new assistant Amy Pond is shaping up to make both of the Doctor's hearts beat faster,' he said. 'Hard-core fans have been moaning on the forums about the danger of sexing up their beloved Time Lord but, thus far, it feels to me like Matt Smith and Gillan are going to get that whole subliminal Mulder and Scully-style passion spot on. Add to that lead writer Steven Moffat's creepy-child obsession and some cracking space art, and it's official: the Doc is hot.'

Sam Wollaston, in the *Guardian*, was pretty impressed, too. 'It may look different from the old planet, but there are all sorts of parallels and similar issues going on,' he wrote. 'Devolution, animal rights, save the star whale, freedom of information, civil liberties, openness, the monarchy, police brutality, North Korea ... Smilers – terrifying mannequins with rictus grins that will suddenly swivel their heads through 180 degrees to reveal frowns when something displeases them – are pure Peter Mandelson,' he wrote.

'There's even Prozac, though it no longer comes in capsule form. Now, when the people learn the miserable truth, they get a button with "forget" written on it, and their memories are wiped clean ... The Doctor dumps her [Amy], says he's taking her straight home, just as soon as they get out of this pickle. But then she majorly makes up for her mistake by seeing what no one else, not even the Doctor, can see: the truth. The people are saved, the children are saved, the star whale is saved; it's all back on with the Doctor. Thank God for that. I would have been sorry to see the end of Amy Pond, even if she is an anagram of mad pony. I like the tweedy new Doctor, all his hair and enthusiasm. But I suspect, like quite a lot of other boys up and down the country, I've fallen totally in love with Amy Pond. It's probably the Scottish accent. And I thought I'd never get over Rose.'

By this time, no one was in any doubt that *Doctor Who*

was in very safe hands. The Doctor, Amy and a simply superb writing and production team were taking it to ever-greater heights. And they could afford to be a little bit cheeky, too. No Doctor is completely the Doctor until he has faced the Daleks, and in the third episode of the new series, 'Victory of the Daleks', the Doctor did just that. Winston Churchill, the great, wartime prime minister, summons the Doctor to the Cabinet War Rooms, during the Blitz, in World War II. There he introduces Professor Edwin Bracewell, who has created robots called Ironsides, which the Doctor immediately recognises for what they really are. But these are Daleks with a difference, painted in five separate colours, denoting Scientist, Strategist, Drone, Eternal and the Supreme.

Initially, the Doctor is unsuccessful in convincing Churchill that these robots, who appear to be serving the British war effort, are not what they seem. However, a Dalek ship is in orbit nearby; it activates a 'Progenator Device', which turns the earthly Daleks nasty. They exterminate a few unfortunates and flee; Bracewell, it turns out, is an android. The Doctor sets off in hot pursuit.

At this point (and not for the only time in the series), the plot gets a little complicated, although it would appear to involve eugenics, a Nazi preoccupation back then. In order to regenerate themselves, the Daleks need the Doctor to recognise them and so lure him to come to

Churchill. Earthlings set out to fight, but for various reasons involving saving the human race, the Doctor is forced to allow the Daleks to escape. Bracewell is convinced by the Doctor that, android or not, he can still do some good, and off they go again, back into deep space. The crack appears again, behind where the Tardis had been.

Again, it went down well. 'It's easily the best that Mark Gatiss has written for the show,' blogged Daniel Martin on the *Guardian* website. 'Facing the Daleks off against Winston Churchill was just always going to be funny, and the idea of them as "man-made" war machines wasn't as heavy-handed as you might have expected. But really, the WW2 backdrop was really just window-dressing for the real story. This was an infinitely better resurrection of the Daleks than the ropey Peter Davison adventure of the same name. It's true that the repetitive thing of them always being the last ever Daleks in the universe was getting implausible. And what fun it is to impose plausibility on a show about time travel! Victory of the Daleks serves as a prologue for something bigger to come – restored and pimped up into a sleek new Technicolor upgrade, they've scuttled off through time to grow in number. And will be back, deadlier than ever.'

Patrick Mulkern, meanwhile, was blogging for the *Radio Times*. 'Gatiss indulges the cognWhoscenti with references to that 1966 classic, 'The Power of the Daleks'

– sometimes shot for shot,' he said. 'Menacing eye-stalk views of the Doctor …"I am your ser-vant!" becoming "I am your sol-dier"… But, as with all the best Dalek stories, there are innovations. First, Bracewell's Ironsides, conniving in khaki, eavesdropping around the Cabinet War Rooms and dishing out tea – and then, thrusting from a Progenitor, a souped-up super race in five collectable colours. It's Invasion of the Dulux! I spy a shameless merchandising opportunity there.'

Mark Gatiss was becoming a very popular writer on the show, much as Moffat had before him. And it was a mark of the faith *Doctor Who*'s producers had in him that they allowed him to get away with such liberties. For a start, the Daleks actually won. How did that make him feel?

'Very exciting!' he proclaimed. 'They've sort of wriggled out of defeat before but I think this is the first time they've got it away with it. Steven [Moffat] was very keen that, with the Time War behind us, the Daleks should simply be re-established as the threat they used to be. That plus the chance to "re-invent" them was just wonderful.'

And, indeed, Mark had been involved in the redesign. 'We talked at the first meeting about making them more like the Daleks from the 60s movies – which I've always loved,' he said. 'The sheer boldness of those colours and the size of them just get to you! So we discussed the idea

75

of a new "paradigm". A template from which future Daleks would spring. Then we had lots of fun coming up with the classifications: Drone, Scientist, Strategist, Supreme and the Eternal. Originally I wanted a green Dalek but green just doesn't seem to work somehow. Funny the things you discover. In the script I put "Big buggers. Bigger than they've ever been." And they are!'

And like so many others involved in the new *Who*, Mark himself was a long-term fan. What would be his favourite? 'My desert island Who is a tough one!' he said. 'For sheer entertainment and brilliance, I've always adored "The Talons of Weng Chiang". Ticks all my boxes as well as being incredibly clever, mould breaking and funny. If it existed, maybe "The Web of Fear", but I suppose I'd have to say "The Green Death". It means so much to me to this day and not just as nostalgia. An eco-story years before its time. Legendary monster ("the one with the giant maggots"). Witty and perfectly Pertwee script. And, of course, that ending. It still makes me cry and completely sums up why I've always loved *Doctor Who*.'

Now that it was so clear that the new Doctor was a real success, Steven Moffat was allowing himself to deliberate on the series. Could the Doctor be thought of as a brand? After all, the new merchandise was selling heavily, and the show was clearly a commercial success. But brand? Absolutely not, according to him.

Steven also had a very strong vision for the format of the show. 'For me, *Doctor Who* literally is a fairy tale,' he said. 'It's not really science fiction. It's not set in space; it's set under your bed. It's at its best when it's related to you, no matter what planet it's set on. Every time it cleaves towards that, it's very strong. Although it is watched by far more adults than children, there's something fundamental in its DNA that makes it a children's programme and it makes children of everyone who watches it. If you're still a grown up by the end of that opening music, you've not been paying attention. You don't think of it in terms of a challenge. You think, "Ooh, wouldn't it be great to do that!" and I'm now in the fortunate position of being able to think that and make it happen.'

Steven was also aware of both the advantages and the dangers of trading off past glories – a very delicate balance had to be struck. 'The more you back-reference, the more it feels like a sequel and the sequel is never as good as the original,' he said. '[But] old favourites can return, provided you can do something new and exciting with them. There are no past characters coming back in this series, but I imagine that kids would love to see Captain Jack meet the new Doctor.'

As a matter of fact, the Doctor was about to meet someone else – River Song, who had already encountered the Tenth Doctor and who might at some stage have been (or will be) the Doctor's wife. She was about to reappear in the next episode, 'The Time of Angels', along with the Weeping Angels, some of the most terrifying monsters to appear in *Doctor Who* to date. The Weeping Angels had originally appeared in the Steven Moffat-scripted episode 'Blink', thought by many to have been the best episode of *Doctor Who* ever made. The extreme malevolence of their nature was summed up by the Tenth Doctor: they are 'creatures of the abstract', 'the lonely assassins', 'the only psychopaths in the universe to kill you nicely', because their touch sends victims into the past to live out their lives before they have actually been born. They are, according to the Doctor, 'as old as the universe, or very nearly, but no one really knows where they come from.' On screen, they have the power to petrify.

The Weeping Angels look like statues (hence their name): their physiology is quantum locked, so that they can only occupy a single position when they are being observed. This means they can't move, but can get about very quickly indeed when unseen, occupying many positions in space. They're a difficult enemy to get one over on, as well – 'You can't kill a stone,' the Tenth Doctor observed – but while in locked state, they often cover their eyes with their hands, in order to avoid accidentally catching one another's gaze and remaining locked in stone forever more.

And this time, it was personal. The episode opened

with the Doctor and Amy rushing to rescue Dr River Song from a starship, *Byzantium*, seconds before it crashes 12,000 years in the past. Deep within the starship's hold is a Weeping Angel, which is getting steadily more powerful as it absorbs radiation from the ship. Dr Song calls on Father Octavian and his troops to help her recapture it and protect a human colony on a nearby planet.

In one of those moves that the viewer just knows is going to end badly, Dr Song produces a four-second video of the Angel. She is left alone to watch it as the other two read a book written about the Angels, which informs them that any kind of image of the Angel – such as a four-second video loop – will turn into the Angel itself. Just as they make this rather worrying discovery, Amy realises that the Angel is moving out of the footage, and as the Doctor frantically battles to break into the viewing room and save her, she seems doomed. Finally, however, she manages to freeze-frame the image, which disappears.

To get to the *Byzantium*, the group then set off through 'Maze of the Dead', a stone labyrinth full of stone statues where the Weeping Angel could be hiding. Two soldiers are left to guard the entrance; the group splits up to explore. It is only when they are in the middle of the labyrinth, absolutely surrounded by Angels, that the Doctor and Dr Song suddenly remember that the natives of the plan, long since vanished, the Aplans, had two heads – and these statues only have one. Belatedly they realise that every one of the statues is actually a Weeping Angel, currently in an extreme state of disintegration due to centuries without sustenance, but now absorbing energy like there was no tomorrow (which there wouldn't be if the Doctor and his cohorts didn't get a move on). It appeared that the Weeping Angel locked away in the *Byzantium* deliberately caused the ship to crash in order to rescue its kind.

Amy, meanwhile, has been having problems, and as the rest of the group flees, she believes her hand has turned to stone, rooting her to the spot. In fact, this is an illusion, and the Doctor gets her moving, before they learn that the Angels have killed their guards and are using one of them, Bob, to talk to the Doctor. They gleefully tell the Doctor they have lured the group into a trap directly under the crashed ship: this time round, rather than sending the group into the past, they intend to kill them and use the energy to regenerate. But they put something else in this trap that marked the fatal flaw in their cunning plan, the Doctor remarked. 'Me.'

It was a high note on which to end the cliffhanger, and the moment at which the Doctor totally exuded the authority and wisdom that goes with the role.

Matters were resolved in the next episode, 'Flesh and Stone' (the title was suggested by Steven's son). The Doctor destroys the gravity globe, thus freeing the assembled company to leap into the *Byzantium*'s local gravity well, and gets everyone into the ships oxygen factory, a forest, with the Angels in pursuit, and with another view of the sinister crack first seen on Amy's bedroom wall. It now appears to be leaking energy, which the Angels are feeding upon.

Everyone makes for the ship's control room, with the exception of Amy, who is becoming too weak to move. There is an image of an Angel embedded in her mind: the only way she can negate its influence is to keep her eyes closed, which in turn makes her vulnerable to the other Angels, as she can't see them. Four clerics are left to guard her, as the Doctor, Song and Octavian move to the ship's control room. The Doctor discovers that Song is actually Octavian's prisoner, with a promised pardon should she complete the mission, although this is soon immaterial, as Octavian dies.

Back in the forest, the ominous crack is opening ever wider; the four clerics guarding Amy go to investigate and disappear. Amy is thus forced to make her own way to the control room, under the Doctor's guidance, walking as confidently as she can in order not to let on that she cannot see. Inevitably, she trips, but is saved as Song teleports her to the control room.

By this time, the Doctor has realised that the mysterious crack, which causes time itself to be unwritten, is due to an explosion somewhere in time and it can only be closed if a 'complicated space-time event' happens: this is achieved when the ship's gravity fails and the Angels fall into the crack. Song is recaptured by the remaining clerics, her crime being to have, 'killed the best man [she'd] ever known' and tells the Doctor they will meet again when the Pandorica opens. The Doctor and Amy return to earth where Amy, in a scene that occasioned much comment, propositions the Doctor, before revealing she is to be married the next day, 26 June 2010 (also the date of the series' finale). The Doctor realises that this is the same day as the time explosion and whisks her out into the stars once more.

Despite a certain amount of tutting in some quarters about Amy's brazen behaviour towards the Doctor (she had appeared to offer the Doctor a one-night stand, greatly upsetting the traditionalists and greatly amusing everyone else), both audiences and reviewers loved it. The plot bounced from one climax to the next; the pace fairly scuttled along, partly courtesy of the mysterious crack, which was clearly going to feature heavily in the climax of the show.

'The overriding feeling I got from this week's episode was one of speed,' wrote Gavin Fuller in the *Guardian*. 'The pace barely let up, as Steven Moffat gave us a rollercoaster ride of thrills and spills, with an ever greater threat than the Angels suddenly rearing its head, while Matt Smith's quick-paced delivery of many of his lines only accentuated this impression. Indeed, despite the visual action, the wordiness given to Smith's Doctor seems to be a key part of this season and looks like being a major facet of this incarnation if the first few weeks are anything to go by. Genuinely one of the most terrifying monsters of the series, the Angels were back here in their full sinister glory, and the staccato way they tend to be shot only adds to their general scariness.'

Dan Martin, blogging for the same paper, went further still. 'I'm just going to come right out and say it. "Flesh and Stone" can lay credible claim to being the greatest episode of *Doctor Who* there has ever been,' he wrote. 'That's better than "Genesis Of The Daleks" and better than "City Of Death" and better than "Tomb Of The Cybermen" and, yes, better than "Blink". It's just ridiculously good – so much that there's scarcely any point in picking out moments because there was an iconic sequence every couple of seconds. Amy's creepy countdown; "I made him say comfy chairs"; the oxygen factory; the clerics being erased one by one; "I think the Angels are laughing"; the moment when the Angel starts to move … You literally have to keep catching your breath.'

Another blogger, Patrick Mulkern, on the *Radio Times* website, felt the same – and was very amused by the amorous note at the end. 'All in all, two episodes of *Who* that deserve 10 out of 10 in anybody's scorebook,' he wrote. 'For me, "The Time of Angels" was marginally more dazzling. Am I alone in finding the decaying Angels in the Maze of the Dead more macabre than their chiselled chums aboard the *Byzantium*? But "Flesh and Stone" bombards us with shudders and tension – especially Amy stumbling through the forest with her eyes closed. I was also much amused by Amy's amorous antics at the end. None of the protracted, doe-eyed mooning of Rose and Martha, or even Donna's classic: "You're not mating with me, sunshine!" Pinging aside the Doctor's braces, Amy isn't "suggesting anything quite so long-term". It seems she's just up for a quickie on the eve of her wedding – or is she actually falling in love with this dorky/dishy Doctor as much as we are now?'

That pretty much summed it up. The hand-wringing continued in some quarters about Amy's immodest behaviour, but the fact was that the Doctor, Amy and Steven Moffat were powering ahead. Or to put it another way: David Who?

CHAPTER 5

WATCH OUT – THESE GIRLS HAVE TEETH

One of the man ways in which the Doctor was thriving in his new incarnation was because of the quality of the monsters. Always crucial in any really good *Doctor Who*, this new lot were as terrifying and mesmerising as anything that had gone before – especially the Weeping Angels, of whom it was safe to say the viewers had not seen the last. Whatever a few naysayers might say about it being too frightening for small children – *Doctor Who* had always been too frightening for small children – the public were loving it. And they were about to get more monsters still.

Doctor Who had always featured monsters that would turn up time and again – the Daleks and the Cybermen being the most obvious examples – but there were also many one-offs, and that was what was to be on offer in the next episode of the series, 'The Vampires of Venice'. There was to be an extra companion in this trip, too.

The Doctor, a little alarmed at Amy's evident interest in him, collects her fiancé Rory, and the three of them set off for Venice in 1580. A plague is running through Italy, so Venice (actually Croatia, but it looked pretty good) has been quarantined by order of Signora Rosanna Calvierri, the city's patron, who runs a school for young women. The fearless trio bump into Guido, a boat builder, whose daughter Isabella attends the school, and who is desperate to know what is happening to her.

That there is something a little odd about the school is not in doubt. Signora Calvierri, her son Francesco and the female students all suffer from some curious traits: they cannot be seen in mirrors, they fear sunlight, and they drink blood by biting necks with their long and very unpleasant teeth – clearly, then, they are vampires. Or so everyone thinks. Amy smuggles herself into the school so that she can let the others in after her; she is caught, however, and taken to a room, there to prepare for vampiredom, before her struggling shows that the Signora is wearing something which allows her to conceal an alien form. The Doctor and Rory arrive and, helped by Isabella, arrange for Amy's escape; Isabella herself, however, still weak in the glare of sunlight, is unable to go with them. She is thrown into the canal, there to be eaten by an unseen creature or creatures that lurks beneath.

At this point, of course, everyone realises that they are not dealing with vampires at all. The Doctor confronts Signora Calvierri and discovers that she and her cohorts are from the planet Saturnyne, alien aquatic beings wearing perception filters, which stop observers from seeing who they really are. That is the reason they can't be seen in mirrors. They fell through a crack in time, of which there were an increasing number on their own planet, and landed in Venice – a good location for an aquatic race – where they wanted to convert human beings into being 'Sisters of Water'. The Doctor goes to Guido to give him the news; a number of the female fishes in human form come to attack them, and Guido blows himself up to save the others.

Signora Calvierri, meanwhile, is set on destroying her new home. She climbs to the top of a tower, and activates something that will start creating earthquakes and tsunamis; the Doctor manages to stop her, while Amy and Rory successfully take on Francesco. Signora Calvierri prepares to sacrifice herself by throwing herself into the canal, there to be consumed by her little ones, but can't resist one last taunt at the Doctor's expense before she goes: he is now responsible for the extinction of two species, she tells him. The Time Lords and her own. And with that the trio repair to the Tardis, there to ponder on what they have just seen.

Again, the critics' reaction was on the whole

favourable. 'If The Vampires of Venice proved anything, it was that this series has significantly raised standards for *Doctor Who*,' blogged Dan Martin on the *Guardian* website. 'It was beautifully shot, and there was plenty to pick apart: the way every part of the vampire mythos was explained away by Who pseudo-science was delightful; the stand-off between the Doctor and Rosanna was beautifully played; the dialogue as cracking as you'd expect from [writer Toby] Whithouse; the Doctor and Amy getting over-excited about there being vampires cute; and the climactic shot of the Doctor scaling the tower in the rain was just the correct level of broad brushstroke.'

Patrick Mulkern on the *Radio Times* site was also impressed. 'The vampire girls are a scream with their bonces backcombed like Fenella Fielding in *Carry On Screaming*,' he blogged. 'I must admit I yawn at aliens disguised as humans. We've seen it so many times now. And Whithouse has used this device in *Torchwood* (Toshiko's lesbian affair with a shapeshifter) and in his nostalgic *Who*, 'School Reunion' (bat-like Krillitanes disguised as teachers). But his script delivers lots of heroics and funny moments for the Doctor, Amy and Rory. A goofy Mr Ordinary, Rory grounds the drama in a way that ethereal Amy can't and is a welcome addition to the Tardis crew.'

But not everyone was impressed. Gavin Fuller, on the

Telegraph website, blogged, 'What we were presented with was a highly derivative romp where a humorous lightness of touch made the threat of the vampires far less effective than it could, or indeed should, have been. The girl vampires acting in unison could have been a memorably sinister enemy, but Matt Smith's Doctor didn't seem to take them terribly seriously, thus negating their effect.'

But his was a lone voice in the wilderness. *Doctor Who* was now dominating the Saturday night schedules: nearly half way through its run, it was as if no one but Matt Smith could ever have been *Doctor Who*.

The writers were pretty impressive, too. Steven Moffat was clearly one of the best ever to have worked on the series, but a veritable (Doctor) *Who's Who* of the best-known names on British television were now queuing up to give it their all. The next episode, 'Amy's Choice', was written by Simon Nye, best known for sitcom *Men Behaving Badly*, and he very much showed himself to be up to the role. His was an intriguing little tale, containing not one, but two, mortal dangers – and a brand new set of monsters, which managed to slot into a tradition created by Russell T Davies. Many of Russell's monsters and aliens had appeared at first glance to be kindly little old ladies or gentle and courteous old men, before they attempted world domination or the destruction of the planet, and so these new monsters were to prove to be.

'Amy's Choice' takes place in two locations: the Tardis and Amy's hometown of Leadworth, five years in the future, where she is heavily pregnant with Rory's baby. The Doctor, Amy and Rory veer between the two realities by falling asleep in one and waking up in the other: they are unable to establish which is the real reality and which is a dream.

It is while they're awake in the Tardis that a mysterious figure called the Dream Lord appears and tells them that they have a choice. They are going to be confronted with two mortal terrors, one real and one not; they must choose which to fight and which to lose. If they choose the real menace, they will be fine. If they choose the false one, however, that will be that.

The two terrors soon make themselves known. In the Tardis power has gone and they are being sucked into the orbit of a freezing cold star; if they do not manage to escape, they will freeze to death. Back down on earth, meanwhile, the older members of the population are beginning to run amok: far from being 80- and 90-somethings tucked up in a care home, they are actually an evil race called the Eknodine, who can kill people just by breathing on them.

Amy's choice is revealed when the Doctor and Rory fall asleep in the Tardis, but she stays awake to be tormented by the Dream Lord. She must choose, he tells her, between a life of peaceful marriage with Rory or excitement with

Doctor Who on the ball. Matt's childhood dream of playing professional football was shattered after a serious injury. However, he soon discovered he had a serious talent for acting.

© *Getty Images*

Top left: Matt enjoys a day out with Billie Piper. The pair acted together, and speculation was rife about whether or not they were an item…

Top right and below: Matt achieved one goal after another while he was still extremely young. After playing in The National Theatre's 2006 production of *The History Boys*, he went on to star in Citizenship, a bittersweet comedy about a teenage boy's search to discover his sexual identity. Matt is seen here with co-star Sid Mitchell.

t the Royal Court Theatre. Matt's role in *That Face* was a turning point in his career.
he entire cast of the play was nominated for the 2008 Laurence Olivier Award for
utstanding Achievement in an Affiliate Theatre, and Matt won the Evening Standard
ward for Best Newcomer in the role. He's pictured here with Julian Wadham, Felicity
nes and Lindsay Duncan.

© *Rex Features*

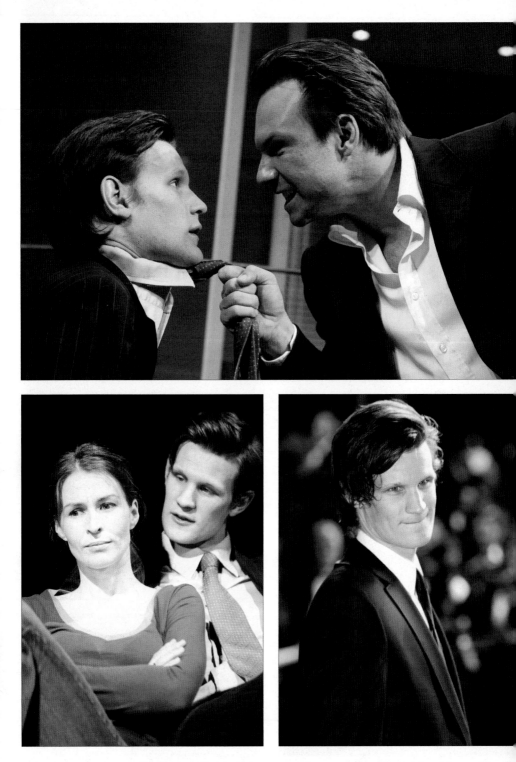

Top and bottom left: Working with Christian Slater in *Swimming With Sharks* was Matt's first experience with a huge international star. 'He's cool,' said Matt. 'He's all about the work…a nice man, a good all round bloke.' Acting with Christian and Helen Baxendale in a long-running play proved a real challenge for Matt – a challenge he relished.

Bottom right: In the limelight at the 2009 Cannes Film Festival.

With actor Harry Treadaway at Sadler's Wells for the launch of the 'Ballets Russes' in 2009. It was while Matt was with the National Youth Theatre that Matt met the Treadaway twins, Luke and Harry, who were going to become two of his closest friends.

© *Rex Features*

The Love Doctor. After a passionate relationship, Matt split from singer and model Mayana (*this page*) in 2009, and has now found new love with model Daisy Lowe (*opposite page*). © *Getty Images*

A new Doctor. After much speculation over who would get the much-coveted role, Matt won the day. He is pictured here with co-star Karen Gillan at the *Doctor Who* serie premiere in March 2010.

the Doctor; her choice will boil down to which world she wants to live in. She then wakes up in Leadworth, where Rory and the Doctor are being attacked by the Eknodine. Rory dies while trying to save Amy, which makes up her mind for her: Leadworth is false and the Tardis is where reality lies. To this effect she and the Doctor ram a camper van into the cottage killing them both; given that all three wake up in the Tardis shortly afterwards, she appears to have made the right choice.

However, there is a twist: this is a dream, too. The Doctor proves as much when he presses the Tardis's self-destruct button and the three wake up for a second time. However, it ends on a slightly subdued note, for while Amy has made her choice – and it is Rory she chooses, not the Doctor – the Doctor is worried about the Dream Lord. The Dream Lord, it transpires, is actually the physical manifestation of the Doctor's darker side – and he will be back. (And for diehard fans, this is not the first time the Doctor has been revealed to have a darker side – in 'The Trial Of A Time Lord', a character called Valeyard appears, who is supposed to have been distilled between the Doctor's twelfth and final regeneration.)

Again, the episode went down very well. 'The choice of Simon *Men Behaving Badly* Nye, with his background in sitcoms, to write an episode of *Doctor Who* might seem at first sight a curious one, but then it's not as if writers with a comedy background have not written for the series before – take Terry Nation for example and look what happened there! (he created the Daleks),' blogged Gavin Fuller for the *Telegraph*. 'And Nye certainly came up with the goods here, with probably the strongest all-round script we've had this year, chock full of good lines, particularly about the Doctor and his attitude to/relationship with his companions, although Amy's line about the prospect of facing death when dressed as a Peruvian folk band was possibly the highlight.'

Dan Martin, blogging for the *Guardian*, called it a 'cunning little character piece.' He said, 'For the most part, it feels like a fun *Shaun Of The Dead*-style romp, all murderous pensioners and lashings of jolly innuendo. Then you get the sting in the tail – and the more accurate reference is *Fight Club* – the revelation that the Dream Lord is actually the Doctor's own self-loathing seems obvious once it's revealed, but also creates the kind of "whoosh" moment that gives a story new gravitas. And the Dream Lord really is deliciously mean, calling him out on his every character flaw; his love of showing off, his clothes, the way he turns people into weapons (to quote Davros), the way he leaves people behind. It's pretty heavy stuff and, at the mid-season point, gives us the first instance of the character opening up and beginning to unravel.'

Over at the *Radio Times*, Patrick Mulkern was initially cautious, in particular expressing concern at the demonisation of old people (although in truth, they make far scarier villains than the young and fit), but softened after a second viewing. 'Nye reinforces the idea that the Doctor is an old man who "prefers the company of the young"; his friends are just "people you acquire" never seen again "once they're grown up",' he wrote. 'Curiously, the Dream Lord and both dream worlds are drawn from the Time Lord's psyche. The Doctor admits the "psychic pollen" is a mind parasite, which "feeds on everything dark in you. Your inner voice. It turns it against you". And Toby Jones is perfect as the Rumpelstiltskin nightmare emerging from the Doctor's paranoia.'

By this time, however, viewers and critics alike were beginning to spot another problem. The Doctor had not one companion but two, and while that had certainly been done before, in this case the companions in question were a couple. And now Amy had chosen which one she preferred. This set up all sorts of potential problems, not least because it risked the Doctor looking like a gooseberry, not something he had ever been before. And then there was the fact that while Amy had made her choice, the viewer didn't necessarily agree with her. The Doctor was a pretty fascinating chap with whom to while your time away around the universe, after all, and Rory's continuing presence was going to highlight the fact that for some people, at least, Amy had made the wrong choice.

This little problem appeared to have been solved in the next episode, 'The Hungry Earth'. Written by Chris Chibnall, a long-standing writer on the series *Torchwood*, it was the first of a two-parter, featuring some monsters last seen way back in 1984, the Silurians, a reptilian race who had been lurking far underground in the barrels of the earth.

As the episode opens, the Doctor, Amy and Rory set off for Rio de Janeiro (which gives an excuse for Amy to run around in a very short skirt throughout the series), but actually land in the Welsh village of Cwmtaff in 2020, where something very odd is going on. A local mining operation, led by Doctor Nasreen Chaudhry, has uncovered minerals that have not been seen for 20 million years. Also present are Tony Mack, a local, his daughter Ambrose and her son Elliot; they are studying another oddity, namely the disappearance of bodies from nearby graves.

At this point the earth opens: Tony is saved, while Amy is dragged underground. But the Doctor has by now worked out that the minerals comprise a bio-reactive defence system that was triggered by the drilling operation; more than that three life forms are making their way to the surface of the earth. (This allows the Doctor one of the best lines in the series: 'You're not just drilling down. Something is drilling up.') Various people barricade themselves in the church and the three retiles appear: in the ensuing fight, one, Alaya, is captured, Tony is struck by a venomous forked tongue, and the other two capture Elliot and disappear. Now both sides have a hostage and negotiations can begin.

Alaya turns out to be a warrior Silurian, awoken from millions of years of deep slumber by the drilling (it was clear at this point that the episode had strongly environmental overtones) and prepared to fight for the return of earth to her race. Rather unfortunately, she begins to taunt the humans, predicting one of them will be the cause of her death. The Doctor, accompanied by Nasreen, meanwhile, enters the Tardis, there to travel to the bowels of the earth. In the meantime, Amy awakens to find herself strapped to an operating table; beside her is Mo, Ambrose's husband, who had been swallowed by the earth at the beginning of the episode. They take on board the bad news that the Silurians intend to vivisect them. The Doctor and Nasreen, meanwhile, discover that far from the small community they were expecting to encounter, there is a vast and extensive civilization peopling the bowels of the earth. And there the episode ends on a cliffhanger – for some reason, despite having been very exciting, the lowest rated episode to date.

The Rory problem, as it were, was solved in the second of the two-parter, 'Cold Blood'. Deep in the bowels of the earth, the Doctor and Nasreen are apprehended by the Silurian and taken off to be examined by a doctor,

Malohkeh. Amy and Mo have already managed to escape and have found Elliot, sedated and under observation. Elsewhere, Nasreen is also sedated, while Malohkeh begins to examine the Doctor, causing him terrible pain until he finally realises the Doctor is not human and desists. Restac, the leader of the Silurians arrives and demands their deaths: they are taken to a Silurian court; Amy and Mo turn up and are captured, too.

However, the Silurians are not all speaking as one. Eldane, Restac's superior, arrives, and demands that hostilities cease. The Doctor gets in touch with everyone still above the earth, telling them how important it is that they keep Alaya alive: unfortunately, however, he is too late. Unable to bear being goaded about Tony, who is developing a very ominous and slightly branch-like green streak where he has been stung, Ambrose has killed her.

Blithely unaware of this disturbing development, the Doctor ploughs on underground. He gets the Silurians and the humans to start talking to one another, negotiating ways in which they can share the earth. He summons the others to come down, unaware that they will be bringing with them a corpse. Nor is that the half of it. Concerned about what will happen when the Silurians learn about Alaya, Ambrose gets Tony to set the drill to burrow further and self destruct 15 minutes after they depart, destroying the Silurian oxygen supplies once and for all.

There are tremors down below, as well. Restac has killed Malohkeh and awoken her fellow warriors, in order to take over from Eldane. She gets angrier still when the humans arrive with Alaya's corpse, but the Doctor manages to disable their weapons temporarily, to give everyone the chance to escape. It is then that he learns the big news about the drill: however, the Doctor and Eldane realise they can disable it using Silurian technology, although that means the only way back to the earth's surface will be via the Tardis, as the exit route will collapse. Eldane deals with the warriors: he gets a 'toxic fumigation' programme to start, forcing them back into hibernation and giving the humans time to escape. Tony decides to stay, as it is the only way his venom wound has a chance of being healed; Nasreen – for the two are in love – decides to stay with him. After all, she can work underground as well as on top of it. Hopes are expressed that, a thousand years hence, humans and the Silurians might actually be able to get on.

The rest get back to the Tardis, where that crack in the cavern wall has appeared again. The Doctor reaches through it and finds something that clearly frightens him (it appears to be a future and decayed part of the outside of the Tardis) but there is an abrupt interruption from Restac, who is dying and wants to take down the others, too. He fires at the Doctor, but Rory sacrifices himself to save him and dies in Amy's arms. His body is sucked into the crack, at which point he ceases to ever have existed, and so despite the Doctor's best efforts to jog her memory, Amy forgets about him. They return to where they had started out to see a vision of Amy walking in the distance. It is the same vision they had had at the beginning – but back then Rory was in it, too.

It certainly deals with the Rory problem (for now) and having had him never exist at all meant there was no obligation for Amy to lower the mood in the next few episodes by being depressed about her lost love. *Doctor Who* has had a tradition of killing off its main characters (although never the Doctor or an assistant). But even so, the abrupt exit of Rory provoked quite a shock.

The critics had their say. Gavin Fuller was not quite as fulsome as usual, pointing out that it harked back to Jon Pertwee's Who in the Seventies, when he had also faced the Silurians, and finding it lacking compared to the original. But it had its moments, he said. 'The most noticeable thing about the episode in general was perhaps how it was the women who were the deadlier and stronger creatures for this episode, with Alaya, Restac, Amy and Ambrose proving the gutsier moments, brandishing weapons and being responsible for all the killings while the menfolk reacted with disgust,' he wrote. 'Plus the sudden swerve at the end, with the return of the crack in the wall and the shock demise of Rory – although I have a sneaking suspicion that all is not what it seems there, allowing for strong performances from Matt Smith and Karen Gillan as Amy comes to terms with the loss of her fiancé, and the revelation at the end of the episode that it appears to be part of the Tardis that the Doctor retrieved from within the crack, making it ever more intriguing as to how this ongoing thread will be resolved.'

Simon Brew, on cult TV and movie website Den of Geek, thought it worked. 'If you were one of the many, like ourselves, who felt that last week's *Doctor Who* had a distinctly old-style tinge to it, then for much of the duration of "Cold Blood", you're going to feel exactly the same way,' he wrote. 'For, to some degree, this was *Doctor Who* how it used to be. Expecting last-minute interruptions to dastardly plans? Running around corridors? The Doctor negotiating and being reasonable with alien races? You get it in abundance here, and that feel of the old Pertwee adventures of old is present and correct. And you get the Silurians too, albeit in greater number than we saw with the story opener, "The Hungry Earth". Not too great a number, to be fair – the Excel spreadsheet is still a little bit of a dampener on ambitions. But not for the first time this run, *Doctor Who* manages to get a lot out of not too much.'

Dan Martin at the *Guardian* also pointed out the parallels with the past. 'Your enjoyment of "Cold Blood" would seem to hinge entirely on whether you've seen a Silurian story before,' he wrote. 'That was certainly the case in my house. With a reptilian gap in my own archive I was all "coo" and "squee", while my older, more encyclopaedic buddy had seen it all before. It's true that all the story's main twists and revelations – humanity's reputation as "the vermin race"; humanity doing terrible things to reinforce that reputation; the Silurians having just the same political divisions as we do – are all present and correct. You have to think of it through the eyes of a child. And I loved this tense, mad and thoughtful story. Especially the bit when they run (again, like giraffes) over the bridge at the end.'

All of this, especially the revelation that the Doctor was holding on to a charred piece of the Tardis, was a clear sign that an apocalyptic end to the series was in sight. However, the next episode, "Vincent and the Doctor", was considerably lighter in tone, and again was written by a very big name in British television and film indeed. Richard Curtis was the man who was to bring together the Doctor and Vincent van Gogh, and he managed to do so in a way that harked right back to his *Four Weddings and a Funeral* best.

The Doctor and Amy are at the Musée d'Orsay in Paris, where another Richard Curtis favourite, Bill Nighy, acting a curator called Dr Black, is holding forth about Van Gogh's genius. He is also, of course, mad, and it is this madness that allows him to see what others cannot. Peering at a painting called *The Church at Auvers*, the

Doctor realises that, just visible in one of the windows, is a painting of an alien. There is no time to be lost. Our heroes get to the Tardis and head back to 1890.

Landing in Arles, the duo finds Vincent, bad tempered, lonely and shunned by all his neighbours; fortunately, however, Amy's womanly charms soon win him round. He certainly needs their help: there has been a spate of recent and mysterious deaths, and it is Vincent himself who is being blamed.

The Doctor and Amy go to stay with Vincent, where it become apparent that he has no idea of the scope of his talent, and is very near to despair. He also is the only person in the vicinity who can see a marauding and malevolent beast. The beast then attacks Amy, so Vincent paints a picture of it: it turns out to be a Krafayis, a vicious pack predator that has been left on earth. There is an altercation: the Doctor and Amy say they will deal with it and go; Vincent breaks down because everyone leaves him in the end.

Still, he manages to pull himself together for long enough to help them confront the creature. First the Doctor enters the church, followed by Amy and Vincent; the beast attacks, at which point the Doctor realises it is blind. That is why it has been left behind. It makes for Vincent, who defends himself using his easel: the Krafayis impales himself upon it and dies.

Vincent is able to understand it now: it was fear that led

the creature to behave as it did. The trio go outside and gaze at the starry, starry sky, from which Vincent is to derive so much inspiration; the Doctor and Amy then get ready to go. Vincent tells Amy to come back and marry him should she ever tire of the Doctor: the Doctor, meanwhile, has an idea. He bundles Vincent into the Tardis and takes him back to the future, in the Musée d'Orsay. Vincent is overwhelmed to see his pictures hanging on the walls, and even more so when he hears Dr Black describing him as 'the greatest painter of them all', a Richard Curtis touch if ever there was one. He kisses him on both cheeks, before being taken back to his own world, greatly cheered.

But Vincent does not escape his fate. Amy and the Doctor return to the present – and discover that Vincent still kills himself, at the age of 37, a year after their encounter. Amy is distraught, but the Doctor comforts her, saying that there is both good and bad in life. Meanwhile, the face in the painting has done – and another painting, *Vase With 12 Sunflowers,* now has an inscription. 'For Amy', it says.

Richard Curtis's involvement ensured that this episode got an even wider reception than usual.

'There's no gainsaying a lump in the throat, though, however treacherous you feel it to be,' wrote Tom Sutcliffe in the *Independent.* 'And this time it wasn't the Doctor who was hauling on the heartstrings but Vincent van Gogh and, behind him, Richard Curtis, writer of an episode that was at first ingenious and then decidedly poignant ... Curtis – having danced a bit of a two-step around the difficult issue of Van Gogh's suicidal depression – gave life to a charitable fantasy that must have occurred to virtually everyone who loves his paintings. The Doctor – unwilling to meddle with history to any large degree – did feel able to take Van Gogh on a temporal joyride, bringing him into 2010, so that he can see the crowds admiring his paintings and hear Bill Nighy's art expert wax lyrical about his undying genius. And in Tony Curran's tender performance of Vincent as he absorbed this fact there was something very touching – one of history's injustices corrected, if only in fantasy.'

Keith Watson, in *Metro*, was similarly affected. 'What would Vincent van Gogh make of the fact that, though he died penniless and unrecognised, he's now regarded as one of the world's greatest artists?' he asked. 'That sounds like the starting point for some kind of earnest talking heads discussion, but no, this was *Doctor Who* time travelling into surprising territory. Taking us into an impressive imagining of Van Gogh's world and his starry, starry night, Richard Curtis's story mixed arch jokes ("Sunflowers? They're not my favourite flower.") with a dark voyage into a tortured life that gambled on a feel-good twist and, against the odds, pulled it off.'

Peter Bradshaw, in the *Guardian*, was also impressed,

although in his case, he commented that it was *Doctor Who* giving a much-needed boost to the career of Richard Curtis, rather than the other way round. 'Richard Curtis is back with a bullet, his mojo apparently restored by one of our great small-screen institutions, and if you haven't yet seen it, then settle down to his terrifically clever, funny, likeable wildly surreal episode of *Doctor Who*: "Vincent and the Doctor",' he wrote. 'In it, the Doctor – played by Matt Smith – notices a strange creature tucked unobtrusively away in one of Van Gogh's paintings ... He travels back in time to meet the great artist, played by Tony Curran, and helps him battle this same scary monster. Curtis induces the soufflé to rise without apparent effort and makes it all look very easy. There are some very tasty Curtis moments. The Doctor exchanges badinage with Bill Nighy's art expert about bow ties. And when he meets Van Gogh, the Doctor becomes very droll and floppy-haired in a way that somehow ... reminds me of someone ...? There is instant comic chemistry between the dapper Time Lord and the shaggy, lairy, wild-haired artist who could almost be played by Rhys Ifans – although Curran is very good.'

Curran was, in fact, excellent, so much so that his performance was singled out for praise by almost everyone who reviewed the show. More than that, 'Vincent and the Doctor' was feted for other reasons as well: it had put the visual arts at the centre of one of its episodes, and it had dealt with the very tricky issue of mental health. When the BBC pulls the stops out, there is no other organisation that can provide better drama. In a series that was already winning plaudits, had introduced a phenomenally popular new Doctor, and was just getting more and more inventive with every episode, this was an unqualified triumph.

CHAPTER 6

THE FINALE APPROACHES

As Matt Smith's first series as the Eleventh Doctor neared its end, the verdict was close to unanimous: he had pulled it off to magnificent effect. David Tennant was about as hard an act to follow as there could be, but Matt had done it; he'd made the role unmistakably his own. But it was a triumph for Steven Moffat, too. Russell T Davies wasn't exactly the easiest writer and executive producer to follow, but Steven had taken the series from strength to strength.

For *Doctor Who* to succeed, there must be a certain amount of enchanting barminess, and this was certainly the case in the episode just before the two-part finale, 'The Lodger', when yet another big name in British entertainment made an appearance. This time it was James Corden, who played Craig, both the somewhat unlikely love interest in the episode and, for a short time, the Doctor's flatmate – for the Doctor's real challenge in this episode is to pass himself off as a normal human being. Luckily for the viewers, he didn't quite manage it.

It was becoming a running joke in this latest series that the Doctor kept managing to land the Tardis in the wrong place, and so it was to prove again. The Doctor and Amy are heading for the fifth moon of Sinda Callista, and instead end up in Colchester (which, let's be honest, required slightly less expensive sets), where problems emerge. The Doctor is flung out of the Tardis, but it cannot land, and Amy is trapped inside. And that isn't the only problem. In a nearby house, passersby are being lured inside by a voice asking for help through the intercom: that is, needless to say, the last that is seen of them. Lights flash, and there is a lot of screaming. A mystery has emerged.

As fortune would have it, the flat downstairs in this mysterious house has a spare room, which the Doctor moves into and where the pretence at being human begins. He is managing to talk to Amy through an earpiece; she in turn tells him how to behave. In the meantime it transpires that Craig is in love with his friend Sophie, who in return is in love with him. However, neither realises the other has such feelings, and both are getting along, rather reluctantly, as platonic friends. Sophie then, to Craig's great dismay, decides to go off to explore the world.

The Doctor starts to become aware that something a little odd is happening in the flat upstairs. A dark stain has spread across the ceiling but the Doctor doesn't want to use his sonic screwdriver to find out what it is in case it sets off an alarm, so he starts to build a rather complicated contraption in his room.

Craig then, rather unwisely, touches the damp patch and is poisoned. The Doctor looks after him, which involves going to Craig's place of work, a call centre, where he does the job remarkably well. He then goes off to play football with Craig's friends – a scene that must have been a particular thrill for Matt, who had been set for a career as a footballer himself until an injury put a stop to it (of which more later) – finally provoking Craig into a huge fit of jealousy. The Doctor is popular, clever, likeable and able, and worst of all, Sophie seems to like him. Craig asks him to move out.

While the Doctor and Craig are arguing, Sophie turns up at the house – and is lured upstairs to the mysterious flat. The Doctor is forced to reveal his true identity to Craig – he does this by way of a head butt – at which point, the two hear screams from upstairs and realise Sophie is in terrible danger. At this crucial moment, Amy reveals an oddity in the building's plans: it has only one storey. The flat above shouldn't be there at all.

The two burst into the flat, which they discover is actually a time machine, which has been projecting a hologram – hence the various mysterious voices. It was a ship that had crashed and rebuilt itself, and was now seeking a pilot to fly it home. All the humans it had enticed inside had been destroyed in the process, but after the Doctor and Craig manage to rescue Sophie, the ship realises that in the Doctor it has at long last found its pilot. It tries to attach him to its energy hub, at which point the Doctor realises that it only seeks people who want to leave, which is why Craig was left alone. Craig and Sophie finally realise that they are both in love and hence want to stay; they touch the ship's console, thus freeing the Doctor. They race out of the house in time to see the flat turn back into a ship and fly away.

Craig and Sophie give the Doctor a set of keys as a parting gift and he returns to the Tardis, which has now finally managed to land. He tells Amy to write a note to be left in a newsagents, directing the Doctor to the mysterious flat in which he has just spent such an eventful couple of days; as she is looking for a pen, however, Amy finds the diamond ring Rory – who she has now forgotten existed – gave her, and looks anxious. The mysterious crack in her bedroom wall appears again. But now it's behind Craig's fridge...

The scene was now clearly set for the series' apocalyptic finale and Gavin Fuller, for the *Telegraph*, was impressed. 'Since *Doctor Who* returned in 2005, episode 11 has tended to be one in which the show draws breath before the grand finale, latterly adding in some sort of setting-up for this in the process,' he wrote. "The Lodger" looked as though it was primed to continue this trend, even to the extent of mirroring the concept of a threat contained in an upstairs room of a suburban house that was also present in 2006's "Fear Her". The trend was largely maintained, but, thanks to the deft hands of Gareth Roberts, it was done in a manner that made the episode a delight. Quite often, small-scale episodes can show *Doctor Who* at its best, and this was no exception, with the menace contained ... to an upstairs flat and the focus of the episode primarily being on the Doctor's impact on his temporarily enforced housemate Craig (a nicely cast James Corden) and Craig's friend Sophie (Daisy Haggard) and showing how the Doctor can, through his perception and wisdom, change people's lives for the better.' It was an apt assessment of exactly why the episode had worked so well.

And so, finally, the big two-parter that was to round off the series approached. It was important for all sorts of reasons: for a start, a really good series of *Doctor Who* has to end so well it leaves the public desperate to see the Doctor back again. Then it was important to establish that Matt Smith was well and truly the new Doctor – not that there was much doubt about that – in a role that he had made entirely his own. Finally, of course, there were all the loose ends to tie up. There was the mysterious recurring crack, the hints of apocalypse – and, to put it bluntly, the audience's appetite for a very strong adventure indeed.

The first of the two-parter was called 'The Pandorica Opens', and it was written by Steven Moffat, clearly keen to leave his final imprint on the series he had made his own. Right from the beginning loose ends were clearly going to be tied up, with cameos from the various characters who had appeared in the series: here was poor Vincent van Gogh, crying out in his madness, attempting to get a message to the Doctor by way of a strange painting that no one can understand; there was Winston Churchill, gruff in the war rooms and working with an equally anxious Professor Bracewell, equally intent on contacting the only man who could save them all. Churchill tries to ring the Doctor, but his call is diverted to River Song, currently languishing in jail; by the clever use of a psychotropic lipstick, she kisses one of the guards and escapes. Next stop is with Liz 10, who is in possession of Van Gogh's painting. It is of the Tardis being blown apart.

Meanwhile, the Doctor and Amy are making their way towards an allotted meeting place. They travel to the oldest planet in the universe to find a message from River: it contains coordinates that send them back to Roman Britain, in 102 AD. River herself is there in the guise of Cleopatra to deliver her warning. The Doctor begins to realise that the destruction of the Tardis might be linked to the Pandorica, something he had previously dismissed as a fairytale and now, rather grimly, is beginning to realise might be real.

And so it proves. The Pandorica turns out to be buried underneath Stonehenge ('Underhenge') and is a prison, a locked room guarded by every conceivable type of lock. Rather worryingly, it seems to be opening itself from the inside; more worryingly still, it is transmitting messages across the universe. Confusingly, Amy declares her favourite story was always *Pandora's Box*, while she has always been obsessed with Roman Britain.

River warns the Doctor that it is summoning all of his enemies, but he refuses to listen, or, indeed, to flee. Rather, he realises that the greatest fighting machine ever invented, the Roman army, is nearby, and goes on to enlist their help.

Back in Underhenge, Amy questions the Doctor about the engagement ring she has found; in his replies, there begins the very faintest stirrings of memories of Rory (who, to recap, had previously been wiped from her mind because, courtesy of the crack in time, it appeared that he previously seemed not to have existed at all). They are distracted by something that starts firing at them: it turns out to be the arm of a Cyberman, which has been severed from the rest of its body. As the two try to escape, Amy is attacked by flailing steel cables, which appear to be attached to a Cyberman's head. It's only a matter of time before the rest of the Cyberman appears, and so it proves: the body storms in, releases the skull of the previous host from the head, and attempts to capture Amy, who just manages to escape. She is rescued by an enigmatic Roman centurion, who turns out to be none other than the previously disappeared Rory – whose reappearance even the Doctor can't explain. Neither can Rory: one minute he was dying, he said, and the next part of the Roman legion. Still, however, Amy can't quite remember who he is.

By this time, matters are getting urgent. The Doctor tries to keep the circling enemies at bay and tells River to bring the Tardis to Stonehenge: instead, she is unable to control it, and finds herself flying to Amy's house on 26 June 2010, the date of the time energy explosion in the universe (and the date of the transmission of the finale). Once there, the scanner shows the same crack in the universe that has been reappearing throughout the series; she hears a voice saying, 'Silence will fall.' River makes her way to Amy's bedroom and finds it full of representations of the Doctor and the Tardis, of Roman soldiers and a copy of Pandora's Box. This is not a coincidence. River and the Doctor begin to realise that their foray into Roman Britain might be something very different: that they have entered a trap, which has been constructed using the contents of Amy's mind.

Everything begins to happen very quickly. The Doctor suddenly realises the date on which River has been taken: he orders her to fly the Tardis away immediately, but she cannot. It is now being controlled by something else. Rory, meanwhile, is finally getting Amy to remember who he is, but just as he manages to do so, it turns out that he and the other Roman centurions are, in fact, Autons. (Autons are another classic set of *Doctor Who* monsters: first introduced to Jon Pertwee's Doctor in the 1970 serial 'Spearhead from Space', they are life-sized plastic dummies animated by the Nestene Consciousness, and quite as dangerous as all the other nasties the Doctor encounters.)

Rory, realising what has happened, begs Amy to flee before he does her harm, but Amy, now that she has remembered him, will not. Unfortunately, he loses control of himself and kills her. Nor is the Doctor having much fun: the other Autons capture him and take him to the Pandorica, which is now fully open – and empty. As Daleks, Cybermen, Sontarans and numerous others gather at the scene, it becomes clear that the Pandorica is indeed a prison – for the Doctor, himself. They all believe that the Doctor is about to destroy the universe; he tries to tell them that it is, in fact, the Tardis that is in danger of doing so, but they refuse to listen and drag him, inexorably, towards his fate. And so the episode draws to a close, with Rory cradling the lifeless Amy, the Doctor about to be shut into internal imprisonment, and River trapped in the Tardis. 'I'm sorry, my love,' she says. The Tardis explodes.

Even for a *Doctor Who* cliffhanger, this was a showstopper. Not since David Tennant's Doctor had been imprisoned by the Master over the course of a previous two-part story had viewers been left so intrigued as to what was going to happen next: the fate not only of the earth but time itself was at stake.

Fans and critics alike loved it. 'Moffat delivers', wrote Michael Henderson, editor of Slice of SciFi website. 'Superb in every sense of the word. THAT is how you do a *Doctor Who* season finale! Ever since the Doctor returned to our screens in 2005, each season of the show has tried to create a season-long story arc, with varying degrees of success. In the first season, 'Bad Wolf' proved to be a fun novelty, let down by its resolution. Part of the problem with the previous season story arc was that the concept of the arc often proved to be far more interesting that the execution and resolution. For all its trying, the new series has yet to have a truly satisfying season finale. Until now… We're halfway there.

'The first words out of my mouth after I picked my jaw up off the floor Saturday evening were, "Now THAT is how you do a season finale!" They were followed by, "Is it next Saturday evening yet?"'

Self-confessed sci-fi geek Eoghann Irving, who had

been following the series on his website eoghann.com, was similarly enthusiastic. '"The Pandorica Opens" had most of the hallmarks of modern Doctor Who season closers,' he wrote. 'Guest appearances from earlier episodes; a threat to the universe etc. But on top of that it had that Steven Moffat style. The snappy dialogue we've come to expect; some heart-wrenching character moments; a story that holds to it's own internal logic and an underlying mystery (to be solved in the final episode perhaps). From the opening scenes as a message winds its way through time from Van Gogh all the way to the Doctor (courtesy of River Song), I was captivated. The pace is fast from beginning to end, but the tone changes ever so slowly as the episode progresses. Starting off as pure action and adventure, it gradually develops darker elements and by the final third I was just waiting for the shoe to drop.'

On IGN UK, Matt Wales was also impressed, all the more so as he had felt some of the earlier episodes in the series didn't quite pull it all off. 'Skirting around the episode's bigger reveals – and there were plenty – "The Pandorica Opens" managed to pack in an absurd number of standout moments,' he wrote. 'From River's message, to the truth about the Pandorica – not to mention Matt Smith's show-stopping speech to the oncoming alien horde – it was all beautifully delivered, if not quite as satisfying as other two-part openers thanks to its wilful evasiveness. And true, the extended slo-mo denouement dipped a little too violently into melodrama but it's hard to fault that bravado downbeat cliffhanger. Indeed, in a season that's largely struggled to spark much emotional investment in its frequently two-dimensional characters, "The Pandorica Opens" really went for the heartstrings. Even among the relentless gobsmacking spectacle, both Karen Gillan and the always-stunning Alex Kingston gave proceedings real soul as their predicaments became increasingly catastrophic.'

There were a few reservations. Was it wise to pack quite so many alien enemies into just the one story? And Rory's reappearance had at that point simply been described as 'a miracle', not, it was generally felt, a good enough explanation for a writer as talented as Moffat. There were also those who said that they had had no problem working out the twist – that the Pandorica was actually a prison for the Doctor himself, surely one of the most powerful beings in the universe, even if, rather than being evil, he was ultimately utterly benign.

But on the whole it was a hugely impressive beginning to the finale. By drawing in so many strands and so many characters that had appeared early in the series, there was a sense of continuity and enormous satisfaction to the fans as the pieces of the jigsaw puzzle finally began to slot into place. And as for the cliffhanger ending: the Doctor was about to be encased in a giant prison that it was all but impossible for anyone to get out of. His enemies had gathered – hordes of them, in every species available. Just how was the Doctor, for all his many and varied talents, going to be able to get out of that?

And so the excitement surrounding the airing of the thirteenth and final episode in the Eleventh Doctor's new series was palpable. Entitled 'The Big Bang', it actually represented a change of tone from the first half of the two-part story in that in lieu of all the monsters gathering, only one Dalek was left, and the plotting was at times so confusing that you needed to be very sharp to keep up. But it wrapped the series up nicely and left the viewers desperate for more.

The opening scene went straight back to the opening of the very first episode: little Amelia Pond is praying for help about the growing and ominous crack in her wall. The Doctor is trapped in the Pandorica, however, and time has been rewritten, so this time he does not appear. But strange forces are at work: when Amelia gets up the next morning, she finds a pamphlet posted through her letterbox, telling her to go to see the Pandorica at her local museum. She enlists the help of an aunt, who goes with her, where Amelia finds another note, this one telling her to stay in the vicinity. She manages to hide until the museum closes, at which point she approaches the Pandorica and touches it. It opens, revealing not the Doctor, but her adult self.

At this point, with time travel responsible for just about every twist coming, the plot becomes complex as never before. Way back, 2,000 years previously, the Doctor had returned from the future to give Rory his sonic screwdriver, which in turn allowed Rory to open the Pandorica and release him. That done, the two of them place Amy's body inside it to preserve her for the next two millennia until her younger self opens it, thus providing the DNA which will bring Amy back to life. In an admittedly extremely touching scene, Rory insists that he will stay with the Pandorica for the next 2,000 years (or, to be accurate, 1,894) to guard it and its precious content; indeed, in the museum itself, a guide is seen giving a speech about the Pandorica and the mysterious Roman legion that was said to have appeared periodically over the thousands of years of its existence, but which had not been seen since the Blitz. Rory is about to reappear, though: Amy and Amelia are attacked by a Dalek, which is shot at by the museum's security guard and thus saving them. The guard is, of course, Rory, still faithfully guarding the treasure that has now been brought back to life. The Doctor appears, having got there using River's Vortex Manipulator to travel into the future; River, and the Tardis, appear to have been destroyed.

Matters promptly get more confusing still. Another Doctor arrives, from 12 minutes into the future, and tells the Doctor in the present to distract the Dalek while he sets up the Pandorica to fly into what appears to be the sun but is, in fact, the Tardis burning up. He has realised that the Pandorica has the power to restore life – hence the newly rejuvenated Dalek – and has worked out that if he flings it and himself into the centre of the Tardis, time will no longer be destroyed and the universe, which is visibly crumbling around them, will come back to life. In fact, it will be a reworking of the Big Bang.

In the meantime, River is still trapped in the Tardis; the Doctor rescues her using the Vortex Manipulator. But increasingly, it is becoming clear that the Doctor is going to have to sacrifice himself to save everyone else. There's still that Dalek to deal with, though: it attacks the Doctor, Amy, Amelia and Rory, shooting the Doctor, who promptly travels 12 minutes back in time. River, showing none of the Doctor's mercy towards others, kills the Dalek, which has still not quite regenerated. She is clearly made of pretty stern stuff.

The Doctor who has just come from 12 minutes into the future has managed to finish rigging the Pandorica, so it can fly straight into the Tardis, and thus touch every bit of the universe through its many cracks. Crucially, before he sets off on his final voyage, the Doctor tells Amy that she has to power to bring people back through the cracks, as she did Rory. With that he flies the Pandorica into the Tardis, and the universe is restored once more.

Initially the Doctor thinks he has escaped once more ('Love it when I do that') until he realises that the only way to close the crack in Amelia's bedroom wall is to lock himself on the other side of it. He revisits every episode in his life as the Eleventh Doctor, ending with little Amelia and his first visit. He picks her up in the garden where she has fallen asleep, having been waiting for him, and carries her up to her bed, telling her a story about a daft old man who had borrowed a really blue magic box which was brand new and ancient at the same time. Then he passes through the crack – and disappears.

The adult Amy wakes up on the morning of her wedding, to find the mother and father she had remembered back to life. As the day progresses, however, she increasingly realises that she has forgotten something very important, so much so that at the reception after the wedding, she finds herself in tears. She catches a glimpse of River walking past, outside. She is given a very blue diary, which is empty. Something borrowed, something blue …

Suddenly, it all comes back and to the consternation of the wedding guests, Amy stands up in the middle of the reception and calls out for the Doctor. The Tardis appears, and the Doctor steps out, in full morning dress, dances wildly and extremely badly at the wedding, and there is much rejoicing all round. Finally, he gives River back the diary, which is empty no longer, and her Vortex

Manipulator, which enables her to go back to her life. The Doctor, Amy and Rory all rush back to the Tardis, where they are summoned – to deal with an escaped Egyptian goddess on the *Orient Express* in space. It is an immensely satisfying and very moving end.

That was it: Matt had done it. He was the Doctor, all right: the role was indisputably his own. Steven Moffat was jubilant. 'I said to everybody else that it would be a minimum of six weeks before he broke through in the role, maybe the vampire's episode, but it was instant for him, right from the debut episode,' he said. 'It was extraordinary. It was like that from the very first reading of the lines. Matt's such a fantastically engaging actor and you don't often get that. He's a ready-made start who pops on to your screen. There's something special that his look brings to Doctor Who too. He's a cool, young guy and old fogey at the same time. He's simultaneously your younger brother and your granddad. He can also seem cool and a geek all at once.'

The reviews were pretty positive, too. Gavin Fuller was impressed – although also a little cautious about giving too fulsome praise. 'This was one of the most high-concept *Doctor Who* episodes ever,' he wrote. 'At one stage Rory expressed his difficulty understanding what was going on, and he might be speaking for much of the audience. Moffat's love of playing with the potentialities of time, evident in several of his former episodes, was evident throughout. Unfortunately, this made the escape for the Doctor somewhat too easy, and rather paradoxical in nature – he only escapes as Rory lets him out once given the means to do so by the Doctor travelling back in time once he's escaped.'

Dan Martin, blogging for the *Guardian*, however, thought it was brilliant. 'Anyway, this was brilliant, wasn't it?' he blogged. 'So brilliant that praising Moffat's event scripts is giving me repetitive strain. Structurally, it was a completely different piece from episode 1 and felt more like a classic *Who* adventure – the team got separated, ran around a bit, found each other, exchanged heroic technobabble and had a jolly excellent time along the way, end of the universe or no end of the universe. Crucially, the alliance of monsters was barely significant; the Daleks being there, without for a moment being all that's there.'

Dan was also beautifully able to beautifully sum up exactly what it was that had made the episode so special. 'We got a lovely whiff of *Charlie and the Chocolate Factory* or *Mary Poppins* in the early museum scenes, from the cinematography as much as the timeless, almost Dickensian child psychiatrist trying to rationalise Amelia's dreams,' he said. 'This was a righteous claim by Moffat to establish *Who* as easily the equal of those classic fables (just, you know, with spaceships). You had to hold your nerve to buy Auton Rory guarding Amy in the Pandorica for 2,000 years, but it was more beautiful just to go with it, and a classically modern fairytale unfolded before our eyes.'

Martin Hoscik, on seenit.co.uk, had previously been a little cautious about the series, but he too loved the finale. 'Wow, that was some finale,' he wrote. 'I may not have enjoyed a lot of Steven Moffat's first series of *Doctor Who* but credit where it's due, he served up a thrilling final episode after a somewhat mixed run. A recurring source of my disappointment has been a "change for change sake" mentality which has peeked out from behind the scenes during *Doctor Who Confidential*, alongside a perceived rush to constantly distance the new run from the multiple-award winning seasons which preceded it ... What the new team have got absolutely right is the casting of Matt Smith and Karen Gillan who have been great and delivered the goods each week despite some ropey scripts. Presumably the new guard have now got running around the office shouting "We're not Russell" out of their systems so they should have a little more time to concentrate on the quality of the series' 6 episodes which fall between the series opener and closer.'

Gerard McGarry, on blogging community Unreality Shout, adored it. 'Oh, readers,' he wrote. 'I've just finished watching it, that final episode. Twice. It. Was. Stunning. "The Big Bang" closes off an incredible series of *Doctor Who*. When we last left the Doctor and chums, they were all in some kind of mortal peril. And within a few short minutes, they're not. It's a brilliant and daring escape that makes not much sense at all, but your head is spinning throughout and the whole thing is laced with mystery and humour. Though we could whinge about the paradox that enables the Doctor to escape the Pandorica, it set up some excellent headsmacking moments. From the outset, we see the Doctor's hand in a million little details – nudging little Amelia towards the museum where the Pandorica is being displayed. And we see the logic behind his frequent reappearances to Rory. Both from when he initially makes them, then from the future, where he's receiving new information from his companions and flipping back in time to tidy up the details.'

And Simon Brew, on Den of Geek, was another massive fan. 'Well crikey,' he began. 'Perhaps we'd all better start by sitting down. For if you were awaiting a simple, easy-to-explain blockbuster of a *Doctor Who* series finale, you simply didn't get it here. Instead, if you were looking for something really very ambitious, often quite confusing, yet ultimately far more satisfying, then "The Big Bang" absolutely hit the mark. Warts and all. For the avoidance of doubt, let's make this clear: we loved it. Even if our head hurts too.'

And so everyone was delighted, all ecstatic with the way the series had been brought to a close. Indeed the biggest complaint about any of it was that viewers were going to have to wait months before they saw the Doctor again. So just who is Matt Smith, this man who brought the legend of the Doctor and his time-travelling Tardis so brilliantly to life?

CHAPTER 7

A TIME LORD IS BORN

Was the curious sound of the Tardis landing echoing in the breeze on 28 October 1982? Did the myriad faces of a 900-year-old Doctor look down knowingly on the balmy autumn night in Nottingham as a little boy made his entrance into the world? There was nothing to hint that one day the newborn baby would achieve greatness with one of the most iconic roles ever on British television – but it was the day Matthew Robert was born to Dave and Lynne Smith. Dave worked in the plastics business; Lynne was to end up in advertising. He had a sister, Laura Jayne, who was to go on to become a dancer. Family life was happy.

An active little boy, Matt had the usual share of falls and tumbles, at one point managing to end up in hospital. 'I cracked that open as a kid at nursery, and had to have 24 stitches,' he told one interviewer, showing off a scar on his forehead. 'Can you see where it goes back?' But his childhood was by and large uneventful, although he did establish a closeness with both parents, especially his father, that was going to stand him in very good stead one day and help him to cope with the price of fame.

Matt attended Northampton School for Boys, where he would one day become head boy, while Laura went to Moulton School. He did all the usual childhood pursuits, including learning to play the piano, and was teased for his angular looks (looks that were to prove extremely photogenic in the years to come), with friends telling him he had a 'face with elbows.' In actual fact, that face, which stood out from the crowd, was soon going to stand him in very good stead.

But it was not acting that interested him back then; it was football. But while that's the case for many teenage boys, Matt went one further than that, for he was highly talented, and at one stage it looked as if football was actually going to become his career. He played for the youth teams of Northampton Town F.C., Nottingham Forest F.C. and Leicester City F.C. 'I played for the Cobblers – that's Northampton Town's nickname – as a kid and dreamed of turning pro,' said the adult Matt. 'Sadly, it didn't happen but I still follow the team and have fond memories of playing in the town.'

Indeed, football was in the family: his father had been a centre back and his grandfather was professional, a striker for Notts County. Matt wanted to be a centre back himself, a dream that came crashing about his ears when he was 16 and badly injured his back. His father ferried him back and forth for treatment at Leicester, and after a year he attempted to go back out on the pitch. But it wasn't the same.

'I could have signed for a lower league club but it was a risk, and the last few games I didn't want to play, I dreaded it,' Matt said. 'I'd lost that desire, the urge, the enjoyment, all the things you need in life. I mean, what's the point in doing something you don't enjoy?'

Actually, Matt was totally shattered by what had happened. Right up until the accident, football had been his life, his future, and his reason for getting up in the morning. It had seemed to be the career path that he would follow, and as such it hadn't even occurred to him he would one day end up excelling in a totally different field. If a person fixates on one subject and one career to that extent and then abruptly has it taken away from them, the effect can be devastating, and that was what was happened to Matt back then.

'I was talking to my dad about it the other day,' he told one interviewer. 'It's the one time … yes, I was in a mess. Football was everything. You think it's the one thing you do in your life, your whole focus … But it's like anything … it's not the disappointment, it's how you react to it. I went to do my A-levels and started doing drama.'

It wasn't quite as simple as that. Matt had grown up thinking he was going to be a footballer. Even after he'd got the role of *Doctor Who*, one of the most prestigious gigs a young actor could hope for, the subject of the football career that never was would come up over and over again. 'It was very tough, though,' he said in one interview. 'I remember crying, because that was all I'd ever invested in. I hadn't really considered acting.' On another occasion, he admitted, 'That was a difficult time. But you know, what doesn't kill you …' In fact, of course, he was even going to be able to put his footballing skills to good use in the episode 'The Lodger', which just goes to prove that few experiences are wasted if turned on their head.

But it didn't feel like that at the time. Matt was all set to become a professional athlete; the realisation that that aspect of his life was over was a very hard blow to bear. Did he but know it, though, the skills he had learned as an athlete were actually going to stand him in good stead as an actor. It would just take some time before that came out. 'There are great disciplines from being a sportsman that you can transfer into being an artist,' he later acknowledged. 'The preparation, the sacrifice, the constant desire to improve.' Indeed, what he had learned in those early days was total professionalism, which was going to work very much in his favour in the days that lay ahead.

It was one of Matt's teachers who saved him, Jeremy Hardingham, whom Matt was later (understandably) to praise to the skies. Jeremy saw that Matt had been all but destroyed by the abrupt end to his footballing career and that he badly needed something in his life to take its place. There are some familiarities between football and acting, both those outlined above by Matt and the fact that both are to some extent a performance on the public stage, so in a move that was frankly inspired, he put Matt's name down as the tenth juror in the play *Twelve Angry Men*. When Matt found out what he'd done, he took part in the play – but it was by no means the case that he suddenly found his new love. Quite the contrary. It took Matt a little while to realise that he'd finally found his métier.

'I had a wonderful teacher called Mr Hardingham, who put my name down for a play without my knowing about it,' he later recalled. 'It was *Twelve Angry Men* and I was Juror Number 10. And then he put me in a drama festival and I didn't turn up, because I was a footballer and acting wasn't that cool. But he kept pushing me and he got me the forms to apply for the National Youth Theatre. I started going to London and spending the summer doing plays with them.'

Gradually, it began to stick. Much to his own surprise, Matt discovered that he loved acting – and was very good at it, too. And so his involvement began to increase. It had felt like the end of the world when his footballing career had been taken away from him – but now Matt was beginning to discover another passion.

Jeremy was thrilled when he saw his protégé was beginning to stand out from the crowd. 'When I first suggested he should try out for a school play he said he wasn't really that interested and had his heart set on becoming a footballer,' he said. 'But just from seeing him in the classroom I knew he had something and I cast him in the play without telling him. As soon as he took to the stage he commanded a certain presence, which made you instantly sit up and take notice. After much cajoling, he slowly started to believe he was good enough to play the parts and really grew into them.'

Jeremy was, in fact, determined that Matt should start acting, and enlisted the help of his mother to get him interested. 'I was head of drama and when he'd done his GCSEs I wanted him to come back and do A-level drama,' he said. We had a new theatre built after the fire and we were doing auditions for a production of *Twelve Angry Men*. I rang his mum and she said he was on holiday so I told her, "Tell him he's got a part in this play and he's going to do it." He didn't have any choice really. His mum and I made a pact that we were going to get him on stage. He did really well in the play and it's like he suddenly said to himself, "Yeah, I like this," and he threw himself into A-level drama. Everything we chucked at him he lapped up. He had a huge hunger to learn and a great work ethic. He was made head boy because he was so popular and a very charismatic young man. He didn't think he'd make it in acting – he was very humble and self-effacing. He was thinking of doing history at university but I persuaded him to go and do acting. He joined the National Youth Theatre and a coachload of students and staff went to watch him in their production of *Murder in the Cathedral*. He was great.'

As for the role he was to take on a few years hence, Jeremy was stunned. 'I was absolutely shocked like everybody else when I realised he had landed the role,' he said. 'Obviously there was a bit of speculation before it was announced but I'm convinced he will be ideal for it. I've known him since he was 14 and even then he was a versatile actor. There are hundreds of kids who pass through school hoping to become a famous TV star and it is really refreshing to see someone who never really had designs on it eventually trying their heart out and achieving it.'

Unsurprisingly, Matt continued to praise the man who had done so much for him. 'He had a significant part in my life,' he said. 'I didn't bother turning up to rehearsals or an audition for a play once, when I was in year nine or ten, and thought I had missed my opportunity. I don't think I was very reliable at the time but he still cast me in that play. He took a chance on me and gave me lots of opportunities and guidance.'

To a certain extent, despite the fact that he was clearly naturally talented, Matt had been very lucky indeed. Truly inspirational teachers can change lives, and so it proved to be in this case. Without Jeremy's determination that this clearly bright and able young man should find another outlet for his energy and resourcefulness, Matt might never have started acting – and the Eleventh Doctor might have been a very different cup of tea, indeed.

And in the eyes of his teacher, Matt's talent was clearly obvious right away. 'He wasn't enthusiastic – he'd done no acting before – but he got the taste for it and he was absolutely fantastic,' Jeremy later recalled. As the Doctor, Matt was famously to repeat the line, 'Bow ties are cool' – back then, he was beginning to discover that acting was, too.

As a matter of fact it was beginning to change his life in all sorts of ways, boosting his confidence and opening his eyes to other possibilities. Matt was really beginning to come into his own. Acting gave him greater confidence, so he decided that he wanted to be head boy, too. He went for it – and won. 'I was the outside choice,' he told one interviewer. 'I curried favour among friends. I just wanted the mantle. I wanted to run things. I wanted control. It was the highest position, and I wanted the highest position. Why not? Then you get to organise the ball and you get to say if you have a yearbook and every Tuesday you go out for a meeting for two hours and get out of triple maths. There was a big hoo-ha with a mate called Dean, because he thought I was using underhand tactics to get votes.' He applied exactly the same determination when going for the role of Doctor, a few years down the line.

By this time, Matt was doing so well as a school actor, that he was beginning to arouse a certain amount of jealousy among friends. One schoolmate was Stuart Robinson, who went on to become a supermarket manager in Swindon. 'We knew each other from 13 years old and had separate friends, but we only really got to know each other in our A-level drama class,' he recalled. 'Matt always had the lead roles in any productions we did. There was certainly plenty of acting talent at the school but it seemed that Matt got all the main roles. I didn't think he was that good an actor – I thought I was just as good as him – but I guess it's down to favouritism sometimes. There was some jealousy.

'Me and my group of friends labelled him Lord Matt of Smithington because he always seemed to get everything. In our A-level performances he would get the main role in the play and we would only get the minor roles. So how can you get marked in your A-level when you're in a minor role? It's unfair. He didn't seem to notice that there were certain people who didn't really like him that much. We got on well and there was a certain level of respect there between us, but it was just the unfairness of it all. It wasn't really Matt's fault, it was just the way he was and the way people thought of him.'

Paul Colliver, who went on to manage an arts-based workshop in Nottingham, also revealed that there was some jealousy at how well Matt was doing back then. 'He got the majority of the starring parts and I remember for the A-level exam piece, *The Venetian Twins*, I was hoping to get the starring role but of course he got it,' he said. 'I was disappointed and a bit miffed, but it actually worked out well for me because I got one of my highest marks. The sixth form was mixed – girls and boys. I think the girls admired Matt more for his acting skills than anything else and I wasn't aware of him ever having a girlfriend there.'

He was certainly going to go on to become popular with girls in the future, of which more anon.

Another classmate was Christian Pinches, who later become a set designer. He remembered Matt as a very lively young man indeed. 'He was one of the lads, that's for sure,' he said. 'I remember he instigated a game where you had to keep a football up and the first person who couldn't do it would get beaten up by everyone else. But he wasn't a bully and he began to mature as the years went on. I remember when he got into acting, in assembly he would perform little acts and warm-ups to advertise the latest show he was in – really in your face – with dramatic moments from the play.'

One of Matt's teachers was Matt Evans, who taught GCSE drama and A-level psychology. He also remembered a very lively youngster, who was so full of laughs and joking that even when he was being serious people didn't always realise it. 'My lasting memory of him was our last-ever drama lesson in year 11,' he said. 'It was the final lesson in our old drama building and we were doing loads of improvisation. I put the light console on full and left the room for some reason. About five minutes later, Matt comes running up the corridor shouting, "Sir, sir, the drama studio's on fire!" You could never tell when he was serious or joking, so I said, "No it isn't, Matt. Now go away." But it turned out he was serious – the whole place was ablaze! He's quite an extrovert, quite a loud character, vibrant and always dominating the scene. He always wanted to answer the question, even if he knew he'd be hopelessly wrong. He's too intelligent to play the fool, but he'd always have a wisecrack to make, which I found endearing. Matt was very keen to impress and wants to please everybody 100 per cent of the time. I used to tell Matt to underplay things when he was acting because he's an extrovert. But I guess you need to be a bit of an extrovert to play Doctor Who so that's perfect for him.'

Meanwhile, Matt had been fortunate enough to meet another inspirational figure who was to play a huge role in his life. The late Edward Wilson was the Artistic

Director of the National Youth Theatre, and an inspiration to Matt, who was beginning to realise that this was where his future really lay. He directed Matt as Thomas Becket in *Murder in the Cathedral*, another seminal experience that was to send him on his way. 'He was a delightful man, he really gave me a springboard and the confidence and the courage to go on and do it,' Matt said. 'So I owe him a lot.'

You could say that again. Although he was not anywhere near ready to turn professional, Matt did so well in the play that he got an agent – and that despite the fact that he was still to go to university, the University of East Anglia, where he was to study drama and creative writing from 2002 to 2005. His work with the National Youth Theatre was also putting him in some pretty starry company: *Murder in the Cathedral* was performed in Westminster Cathedral, and members of the audience included Prince Edward, Sir Ian McKellen and Simon Callow. It was heady stuff. 'The great thing about the National Youth Theatre is the support it has from actors,' said Matt as an adult. 'It is a marvellous platform for young actors and I would encourage any young people to apply. I've met hordes of people through it.'

It was while he was with the National Youth Theatre that Matt met the Treadaway twins, Luke and Harry, who later became two of his closest friends. 'You're only 18 so they give you this pep talk about not having sex with anyone,' Matt recalled, tongue firmly in cheek. 'I was leaning out of the window, and then from the room opposite, this head appeared, having a fag. It was Harry. Then the head of this other twin, Luke, appeared. We've been friends ever since; it's like a little collective.'

It was while Matt was at university that he was to meet the next inspirational teacher who would change his life – his tutor, Jon Hyde. Some years later, when it was announced that Matt was about to take on his iconic role, Jon was thrilled, and remembered his old pupil fondly. But he was as surprised as everyone else.

'I just tuned into the television like everyone else. I was really gob-smacked when I saw this young chap that I'd worked with for three years sitting there in the studio, talking about being the new Doctor Who,' he said. 'It was very exciting. I didn't even know Matt was in the running; they kept it pretty secret. All of a sudden, there he was. This is a great achievement and I am absolutely delighted for him. He was a very dedicated student, very inventive, determined, and you could see he was hugely talented. He is a bright young man and a brilliant comic actor particularly. He had a lot of friends, and worked hard.'

That talent for comedy was one that was to surface time and again in the role of Who, but during his time at university no one knew where it could lead. Matt was proving to be an outstanding student, however, very quickly proving to be one of the leading talents of his year.

'I directed him here in his second year for a play,' Jon continued. 'He was very inventive, very lively and he'd always come to rehearsals with new ideas. The play I worked with him on was a comedy, so I know he has a comic gift as well. I think his character will therefore be quite amusing. He has very distinctive features and he's very handsome. I think a lot of young ladies will be pleased he's the new Doctor once they start seeing him in the spring of 2010. With his looks I don't think he will frighten any of the public, but hopefully a few monsters – he is more than 900 years old after all! I'm very proud of him and everyone here at UEA drama is delighted.'

Matt was attracting serious attention, now – and he hadn't even left university. He continued his work with the National Youth Theatre and landed another role that was to stand out: that of Bassoon in *The Master and Margarita*. By this time it was apparent that a serious talent was on the rise. Although he was still at university, Matt was now to turn professional, in a play called *Fresh Kills* at London's Royal Court Theatre in 2004. From there he went on to take part in *On the Shore of the Wide World* by Simon Stephens, a drama about three generations of the Holmes family, in Stockport, in the north of England, which began at Manchester's Royal Exchange Theatre and which transferred to the National

Theatre. Matt played Paul Danzinger, while the play itself went on to win the Laurence Olivier Award for Best New Play in 2006. It was ironic that when Matt was cast as Doctor Who there were so many people demanding to know who he was, because as a young actor studying drama he was already leaping ahead of the rest.

Matt was now so busy professionally that it was affecting his university work, which meant that he had to come to an arrangement with East Anglia: they agreed that he could graduate without attending lectures in his last two terms. Given the amount of professional experience he was now acquiring, this was an understandable move.

'[*Fresh Kills*] took me out of college for six weeks,' Matt later recalled. 'Then I was invited to appear in *On the Shore of the Wide World*. I said to them [East Anglia], I want to be an actor so you've got to let me go and do this. I didn't go to any more lectures, but they let me graduate. I would get the reading list and do my work and send it back to them.'

It was a good move. Working at the National Theatre meant that Matt met the powers that be, made the contacts that would stand him in good stead and landed another really good part almost straight away. It was that of Lockwood, in Alan Bennett's play *The History Boys*. 'On the first day of rehearsals, [director] Nick Hytner told us how lucky we were,' said Matt. 'As he said, "Not many boys at your age get to be in a play this successful that's at the National Theatre and by Alan Bennett."'

That was putting it mildly. Alan Bennett is one of the most popular and successful playwrights writing in Britain today, and *The History Boys*, which premiered in 2004, made a huge impact when it was first produced. It is set in Cutlers' Grammar School, Sheffield, a boys' grammar school in the north, and centres on three history students preparing for their Oxbridge entrance exam. They are being taught by three teachers: Hector, an eccentric but inspirational teacher who is later discovered fondling a pupil; Irwin, a cynical supply teacher; and Mrs Lintott. Irwin's hidden homosexuality also begins to emerge.

The drama, which won the Evening Standard Award for Best Play, along with an Olivier Award, Drama Desk Award, New York Drama Critics' Circle Best Play, Outer Critics Circle Award for Outstanding Broadway Play, and Tony Award for Best Play, also boasted some stellar cast members, who were either already famous or going to go on to great things. Clive Merrison, Richard Griffiths, Frances de la Tour, James Corden, Dominic Cooper, Russell Tovey and Andrew Knott were among the original cast; initially the play had a limited run, but it was extended time and time again.

The reviews were sensational, too. 'Nothing could diminish the incendiary achievement of this subtle, deep-wrought and immensely funny play about the value and meaning of education,' wrote Michael Billington in the *Guardian*. 'What is astonishing is how much territory Bennett manages to cover: the teaching and meaning of history, inflexible and imaginative approaches to education, and the idea, as *in Forty Years On*, that a school has the potential to be a metaphor for English life. It is no accident that the play is set in the eighties, when the arguments between beleaguered humanism and pragmatic functionalism were at the very height.'

In all, Matt could hardly have managed to appear in a more high profile, wildly praised production, and even if he wasn't in the original cast, it began to give him a taste of what real success could be.

This wasn't the end of Matt's association with the National: he also appeared in *Burn*, *Chatroom* and *Citizenship*. 'As a young actor, there is no better place to learn your craft,' he recalled. 'I remember saying to my dad at breakfast once, "I'd love to work at the National by the time I am 25." I got there sooner!' Indeed, he was achieving one goal after another while he was still extremely young.

The upward trajectory continued apace. Matt went on to make his West End debut shortly afterwards in a play called *Swimming with Sharks*; its star was none other than Christian Slater. Matt had a not totally successful first audition but was recalled and got the part. 'I did better on the recall,' he remembered. And how was it to work with Slater? 'Not daunted, but excited. I love *Heathers* and *True Romance*. And he's a really good guy – a nice bloke. He's funny and genuinely makes me laugh. Yes, I play a bright, enthusiastic young man who is pushed to a very dark, sour place. It's reminiscent of Faust; it's about someone who sells his soul to the devil by the end of the play.'

The play got slightly mixed reviews. Slater played a foul Hollywood producer, Buddy Ackerman, in a play that was based on a 1994 film, with Kevin Spacey in the leading role. He provokes Guy (Matt) to such an extent that by the finale, he ties Buddy to a chair and tortures him, not an easy scene to watch or play. 'Slater's Buddy presides over a studio division dealing in populist slasher films; Matt Smith's rumpled, eager film buff Guy comes to work as his assistant, a job which, his departing predecessor pronounces, involves "a lot of shit work for shit wages",' wrote Sam Marlowe in *The Times*.

'Enter Helen Baxendale's sassy but serious independent producer Dawn Lockard, with a high-minded script called *The Afghani Incident* that Buddy might be able to turn to his advantage, and a hot body he is even keener to get his hands on. A triangular power struggle ensues, as Guy and Dawn fall in love and Buddy plays puppet master. The play toys with notions of dumbing down and artistic responsibility, but never properly engages with them. Nor does it fully succeed as a thriller, largely because it's so difficult to care about the megalomaniac Buddy, the geeky Guy who gradually mutates into a less compelling version of his boss, or the latter's improbable relationship with Baxendale's Dawn, whose attraction towards such a dweeb is almost impossible to credit.'

Lizzie Loveridge, on CurtainUp.com, was none too impressed, either. 'Christian Slater appears rather stiff in the part and his vocal range seems not to vary enough in a stage setting,' she wrote. 'He is content to shout at his victim rather than to mercurially switch from malignancy to opportunism but he does pace the stage like a bear. He is facially impassive, as if his suspiciously smooth forehead had been frozen to fill out the wrinkles. This could be in character as Buddy Ackerman might be the type to employ Botox! Matt Smith looks like a klutz initially but I really didn't care enough to want him to overcome the ghastly Buddy. We know Helen Baxendale has real acting balls, but the role of Dawn doesn't give her much opportunity to show her full talent and Dawn and Guy seem a very unlikely couple.'

Perhaps unsurprisingly, given that mauling, Matt was a little circumspect about the whole experience later on. 'He's cool, Christian, I liked him,' he said. 'He's a good guy but I had a tough time ... for a variety of reasons. I'd never done that length of run before. At the Court, you're in, you're out. So it was quite at a learning curve.'

At any rate, it also gave Matt his first experience of working with a huge international star. He and Christian actually got on very well, which made up for some of the difficulty. '[Christian is] great fun,' he said in another interview. 'He's cool as fuck. He's all about the work; he's really focused on the work. He made that whole transaction very easy. He's a nice man, a good all round bloke.' There was that word, 'cool' again – and a rare incidence of Matt swearing – he was obviously a man who was very aware of what was a little bit stylish, and what worked and what did not.

It also gave Matt some experience of negative reviews, something every actor must get used to, no matter how good they are. As it happens, Matt was going to get sensational reviews when he finally started playing the Doctor, but the run up to it all was something else. He was forced to endure constant criticism about being too young, too geeky, too unknown, too not David Tennant, but he was able to withstand it because he'd had to put up with a lot of stick before.

It was now that Matt started to get some television work. A few years later, when he got the role of Doctor Who, there was wild excitement when it emerged that he had, in fact, previously acted with one Billie Piper – quite a few times, in fact. Billie was playing the lead in the BBC adaptations of the Sally Lockhart Quartet books, although at the time of writing only *The Ruby in the*

Smoke and the *Shadow in the North* had been made; Matt now managed to get the part of Jim Taylor in those two, his first ever appearances on television.

Sally Lockhart (or Veronica Beatrice 'Sally' Lockhart) is a fictional character in a series of books created by the children's author Philip Pullman. She first appeared in *The Ruby in the Smoke*, a play written to be performed in schools, about a 16-year-old girl, Sally, who starts to investigate her father's death. She soon discovers that he is connected to the opium trade, the Indian Mutiny, and a cursed Ruby, and Philip was so taken with his creation that he wrote four books on the back of it, which became known as the Sally Lockhart Quartet, the two already mentioned plus *The Tiger in the Well* and *The Tin Princess*.

Sally herself is the main character, obviously, a very intrepid girl who manages to become a financial consultant, not an obvious career path for women in the 1870s, making various friends and alliances along the way. One of these is Jim Taylor, a Cockney ragamuffin, who loves the theatre and is able to see a person's true worth. In *The Shadow of the North*, he falls out of a window trying to save Fred, Sally's lover and the father of her child, leaving him with a limp for the rest of his life.

The Ruby in the Smoke aired on television in 2006 and met with a mixed response from viewers. 'I feel this would have done very well as a television series, but as a film it merely felt rushed,' blogged indigoharmony on imdb.com. 'The characters introduced promised to be interesting, but weren't really properly developed, and I had trouble keeping up with all the twists in the plot, which were rushed by in seconds. Sally seemed like a fascinating character, but her character development was left to a few scenes of her standing up to her aunt and demonstrating her ability for dealing with figures. This left the film feeling somewhat sterile – more of a puzzle than a story.'

Another blogger, hesketh27, was more positive, however: 'This Victorian melodrama proved to be very enjoyable, perfect for Christmas-time viewing. It was sometimes hard to follow, but the superb period detail and larger-than-life characters more than made up for this. High production values were evident throughout and *The Ruby in the Smoke* stood head and shoulders above the BBC's absolutely dreadful adaptation of *Dracula*, which ran the following night. Good performances from the cast overall.'

Bob the moo was a bit down on Billie, and also on Matt. 'It doesn't really hang together though, as the mystery tends to have peaks and troughs even across the comparatively short running time,' he blogged. 'The central thread concerning Mrs Holland and the ruby is engaging but the rest is not so good and seems to ask the audience just to go along with it. A part of this failing can be laid at the feet of the cast. Piper in particular seems very bland and uninteresting throughout. She had a bit of something about her in *Dr Who* but here she seems to be restraining it as part of her character – which is an approach that doesn't work. In the words of a far less kind commentator – she appears to spend more time focusing on keeping her upper lip pulled down over her big teeth! Walters is much better in her role and her parts of the film are easily the strongest and more enjoyable. Smith is a bit too cheeky chappie for my liking, while Field, Anderson, Gilet, Maudsley and others are all solid enough in their roles.'

The Shadow in the North, which aired the following year, didn't fare much better. 'The Sally Lockhart mysteries proved to be a mild disappointment,' blogged Mart Sander. 'They are not up to the usual BBC period drama standards – or rather they haven't gotten the period drama treatment. The story relies heavily on a Victorian atmosphere, but you rarely get this in the film adaptations. First of all, Miss Piper, lovely and talented as she is, has the least Victorian beauty imaginable. She is so much AD 2000 that every scene with her in it loses every kind of credibility. ...Miss Piper walks straight out of 2007 and makes everything around her 2007.'

LouE15 had actually enjoyed the first drama, but didn't much like the follow-up. 'Maybe it was watching this with my parents when it aired over New Year on British

TV – but I found this strangely detached, even a bit mechanical,' he blogged. 'This time round the leads' chemistry seemed to be absent, the script dry, the story rushed (as was the previous one) – the relations between the characters insufficiently explained. Considering we'd had to wait a year for this one, I was a bit disappointed. Perhaps the aim was to make a classroom-suitable programme for Victorian history lessons? – if so, why air it post watershed?'

And then there was Peter Boots, who certainly didn't mince his words. 'It is sad when an excellent cast is wasted in something quite as preposterous as this,' he began. 'Imagine a late Victorian London where a near teenage young lady styles herself as a "Financial Consultant" and sinks a retired school teacher's entire retirement savings in a shipping line that goes bankrupt after its ship – apparently the only one – mysteriously disappears at sea on a calm day.' There was a lot more along the same lines – he clearly wasn't a fan.

So, Sally Lockhart was to be no Doctor Who, on television, at least. But again, it didn't matter, for Matt was learning his trade. Acting on television is different from stage acting, and he was learning the tricks and how to go about it. And it would shortly be standing him in very good stead.

CHAPTER 8
THAT FACE

It was *Doctor Who* that was shortly to catapult Matt into the stratosphere, but if truth be told, he was doing pretty well anyway. More and more juicy roles were coming his way, including another one with Billie Piper, which got the critics even more worked up than they had been before once it was announced that he was going to be the new Doctor. This wasn't just any old role: it was a part in the infamous series *Secret Diary of a Call Girl*. Now here really was a turn up for the books: the Doctor making free with a previous assistant. It was all very rambunctious stuff.

Secret Diary of a Call Girl had become something of a *succès de scandale*. It had had started as first a blog and then a book by a high-class lady of the night, known only (until she was unmasked as the scientist Dr Brooke Magnanti) as Belle de Jour, after the famous 1960s film of the same name starring Catherine Deneuve and directed by Luis Buñuel. When it was adapted for television, starring Billie Piper as Hannah Baxter, a seemingly normal woman who in fact works as a prostitute, there was a certain amount of shock, not least because Billie seemed extremely clean cut. After her early years as a pop singer, she had become best known first for her marriage to Chris Evans, and then for her role as Rose Tyler. She certainly wasn't the sort of person you'd expect to go around posing as a lady of the night.

The series was never exactly mainstream; it was shown on ITV2. But it garnered a fair bit of interest. Like *Sex and the City*, to which it was sometimes compared, *Secret Diary of a Call Girl* frequently treated sex as more of a laugh than anything else. Billie/Hannah/Belle was the narrator of the series, and would frequently address the camera directly as she came to terms with the fact that she was having a career break. 'Now that I'm not working I'll have to find something else to occupy my time,' she mused, before addressing the viewer with her next conundrum. 'More importantly, I'll have to start giving it away.' Although the show was obviously very different indeed from the one that was to make him famous, it also gave Matt the chance to display his flair for comedy and lightness of touch.

Billie herself was very much a fan of Matt, and was enthusiastic when it was announced that he was to be the

Matt and Karen on set with the iconic Police box. 'It was a gamble to cast a relative unknown, but it's paid off spectacularly,' said a BBC insider.

Matt's new role has kept him busy both on and off set.

Top: Matt speaks to fans the The Apple Store's 'Meet The Cast' event.

Bottom: Greeting young fans at a photocall in Manchester.

att brandishes the iconic sonic screwdriver on *Friday Night With Jonathan Ross*.
he implement's near-magical powers have got many a Doctor out of sticky scrapes.
nset) The screwdriver in action during filming in Cardiff.   © *Rex Features*

Top: A disshevelled Matt filming with Karen Gillan, who plays Amy, the Doctor's assistant

Bottom: Matt has brought a quirky freshness to the role which has delighted fans around the world.

Matt and Karen's on-screen chemistry is intense, and naturally many have wondered if there might be any off-screen romance. But Matt has always insisted they are just great friends.

© Rex Features

Matt and James Corden take a break from a busy filming schedule. 'I think you work so hard as the Doctor on *Doctor Who*, you don't really get time to be in the public eye,' said Matt when he got the part. Little did he know…

© Getty Image

Top: Wherever Matt goes, the fans follow. Pictured outside Radio 1, Matt autographs
way for his faithful followers.

Bottom: Out with Karen for another screening – this time at BAFTA in London.

A star is born. Matt confidently strides into the limelight. His fine acting skills have deservedly won him legions of fans. Who knows what the future may hold for this bright young actor.

Eleventh Doctor. 'I've worked with him three times, including *Secret Diary of a Call Girl* where he was a punter,' she said. 'I love Matt Smith. I think he's amazing and he's a great choice for the new Doctor Who.'

Matt's appearance in *Secret Diary* was brief, but memorable. His character had carnal relations with Billie's Belle de Jour, of course, but unusually, it was not as a paying client, or punter, as Billie had termed him. The two met in a store, where Matt's character Tim was working as a shop assistant and Belle was looking for a wedding gift, before ending up in bed together. The twist to this one was that when they woke up the next morning, Tim wouldn't leave, and because their arrangement was a traditional one, rather than a deal that involved payment, Belle couldn't tell him to do so.

Offering to make him breakfast, all she can find in the kitchen is champagne and a couple of bags of pasta; Tim, meanwhile, having been told she's a legal secretary, finds a cupboard full of massage oil and jumps to the conclusion that she is, in fact, a masseuse. In desperation, Billie rings a male friend, who comes round and pretends to be her fiancé, one who wants to join in the fun. Tim leaves shortly afterwards.

It was a brief role that would probably have been instantly forgotten were it not for the greatness ahead: as it was, the papers were beside themselves when it came to light, full of headlines such as 'Doctor Oo-er.' Matt laughed it off. It was intriguing, though, that the two had a *Doctor Who* connection, and who better than Billie (and David Tennant) to tell him about what lay ahead? Had she talked to him about it?

'Very briefly,' said Billie. 'I don't really know how to prepare someone for that. Basically your entire life changes, and it's really hard. It's also great but you can no longer go to McDonald's and get a Happy Meal. You are followed everywhere. Life is so different and it will be for him. Even going to grown-up events changes. It's all people want to know about. It dominates every single dinner party and wedding. People are obsessed with *Doctor Who*. It's so funny.' The message was the same from her as from everyone else: you simply cannot imagine how your life is going to change.

Of course, Billie herself had had to deal with the constant attention that went with playing a part in such a high-profile series, and so it was that after the announcement of Matt's Doctorship, a set of pictures surfaced that had been taken back in 2006. They showed her walking hand-in-hand with none other than Matt, at a fête. Both denied point blank they had been anything more than friends, but Billie had just split from her husband, DJ Chris Evans, and tongues were bound to wag. And whatever the reality of the situation, they were clearly getting on pretty well with one another – 'Doctor Oo-er', indeed.

'They were very touchy-feely and seemed really at ease with each other,' said an observer at the scene. 'Everybody assumed they were a couple by the way they were acting. A lot of people were talking about how good they looked together. They were definitely having a great time. Obviously, everyone knew who Billie was – but Matt wasn't at all famous then. It's amazing to think he has gone on to star in *Doctor Who*.'

But that was still ahead. Matt was still very much a stage actor, as well as a television one, and now came a role that brought him real acclaim. Although he had been doing very well already, this was the part that made him stand out, that got interviewers interested in him for the first time and that made it apparent he was going to be a great deal more than just any old actor. He was to win acclaim, awards and be forced into a complete on-stage breakdown by the end of it all, and the fact that he made such a huge success of it bespoke major triumphs to come.

The play was called *The Face*, written by Polly Stenham; Matt played Henry, the son of an alcoholic, Martha, who in turn was played by the veteran actress Lindsay Duncan. Felicity Jones played Henry's drug addicted sister, Mia. The play opened at the Royal Court, a theatre with which Matt was becoming pretty familiar, and a year later went on to transfer to the Duke of York's Theatre in London's West End. It was this role that, as much as *Doctor Who*, was the making of Matt. The latter was to make him famous, but this role showed his true scope as an actor, one with still very little experience, comparatively speaking. He had to give emotional depth to a character on the verge of a breakdown and had to explore the darkest sides of a mother/son relationship. It was a huge challenge.

The play was very much a drama for our times. It involved a middle-class family, in which the paternal figure has left, in this case to go and live with a second family in Hong Kong, leaving chaos in his wake, along with destructiveness, disintegration and mayhem. It dealt with drug addiction and alcoholism, and was deemed to be all the more shocking because it was not set in a sink estate but in a wealthy middle-class family, of the type somehow deemed to be above nastiness such as this.

It brought Matt massive attention, put him in the big league and, again, gave him the chance to work with a very big name, in this case Lindsay Duncan. 'I completely admire her,' he said at the time. 'She's a constant source of information — not only about acting but about life and love. She's a cool cat. There's something very rock'n'roll about her.'

Lindsay was equally effusive in return. 'Oh there just aren't enough good words to say about Matt,' she said. 'He's amazing, and he's the most gorgeous person, and I will really treasure being on stage with him, always, because he's so special.' So there it was – not only was Matt a great actor, but he was a nice guy, professional and very well liked by his peers. There was no ego in the making, no monster lurking behind the goofiness here. And given that he was still so young, this could so easily have gone to Matt's head, but clearly, it did not.

The play itself was a searing indictment of a dysfunctional family, in which the children are forced into caring for the parents, and alongside the drinking and alcoholism, Mia, who is 15, starts selling drugs at school – the school is also a very elite boarding school (of the type the author attended), and not the kind of place where you would expect nice middle-class girls to start dealing in drugs.

The character of Henry, meanwhile, is withdrawn, friendless, attempts to look after his mother to the point of becoming totally obsessed with her – and not in a good way – and sees matters go from bad to worse: it was not an easy role to play. On top of that, Henry ends up wearing his mother's clothes and jewellery on stage, and wetting himself in protest at her behaviour. In the final scene Henry's mother dresses him in a silk negligee, pearls and lipstick, much to the horror of his father Hugh, who has finally turned up. Matt later admitted his own mother had found it difficult to watch, which was hardly surprising, given that members of the audience found it very uncomfortable, too.

That was not surprising: there was an incestuous edge to the way in which mother and son were so strongly bound together. Neither could break free of the other and in the end, when the mother finally attempts to do so, Henry falls apart. 'In big, broad, dramatic terms it's about co-dependency and addiction,' said Matt. 'They're [Martha and Henry] completely intertwined together, they are completely united. And it's about that separation and it's about the bombs that go off in this family home that shatter all the relationships. I sort of view it as you would a man who is addicted to crack, cocaine or heroin, whatever – with Henry and his mother, it's that obsession. Their world is kind of defined by each other.'

Although the play confronted very difficult issues, Matt was happy to tackle them straight on. It was a world away from his comfortable, secure family background, and so he could have had no personal experience of the torment his character suffered; it was a mark of what a fine actor he was becoming that he gave such depth to the role. 'The thing I find tricky to get my head round is why doesn't he just leave?' he said in an interview at the time.

'An awful lot of it is co-dependency. So as part of our research we went to meetings where we met alcoholics and people who are either married to them or are alcoholic's children. With Henry there's a real belief – or denial maybe – that he can change his mother. When she is finally pulled away from him to go to rehab, his identity collapses. His sacrifice has been for nothing.'

It was gruelling, though, to go out on stage and display such naked emotion night after night after night. 'After the first run-through, Lindsay and I turned to each other and said: "How are we going to do this eight times a week?"' Matt said. 'And on Wednesday matinees? Fucking hard! Because you just have to pour your whole body, your whole heart at it. And just run as fast as you can. I'm going to have to be disciplined. I'm going to have to drink less. No pints after work...' Not that he had ever shown any signs of not being disciplined previously. Those early years in which he'd trained as an athlete were really coming into their own now: Matt knew how to focus and was doing so to enormous effect.

That Face was a turning point in Matt's life. The entire cast of the play was nominated for the 2008 Laurence Olivier Award for Outstanding Achievement in an Affiliate Theatre, and the role won Matt the *Evening Standard* award for Best Newcomer. His peers were talking about him, and while his name might still have been relatively unknown outside the theatre-going public, aficionados and fellow stage folk were beginning to know who he was. He was still a very young man, but was finding himself more talked about than stage veterans twice his age.

After its extremely successful run at the Royal Court,

there was a brief pause before the play transferred to the West End. Matt had had a break from all that angst up on stage – but was now going to revisit it. He was looking forward to it, however, and had created all sorts of scenarios in his mind about what the unfortunate Henry did next. 'Do you know a band called Antony and the Johnsons?' he asked one interviewer. 'I think Henry will probably turn out making a pained musical album like that. I don't think he'll have sex for a long time. I think Henry's in trouble, he'll have a lot of therapy, and I think he'll struggle with his future relationships. But then, I don't know. We'll see. Maybe Polly will write a sequel. Fingers crossed she does. She's only 21.' Matt was only a couple of years older himself, but was showing a wise head on young shoulders. Clearly he had been giving the role a great deal of thought.

The cast had changed slightly in the transfer to the West End: Hannah Murray was taking Felicity Jones's role as Mia, which in turn gave the cast a chance to look at the play in a slightly different way. 'You can slightly feel sometimes like you're inheriting something and actually it's more interesting and rewarding, I think, to do it through innocent eyes, as it were,' Matt said. 'You sort of question the new choices you're making because you think, actually it worked like that, so why is it not like that now? Obviously we're in a new space and that makes it completely different.' Apart from anything else, the new space was bigger. The Royal Court is a small theatre, which meant the audience got a very intimate view of the proceedings on stage; the new place was larger, which meant that the claustrophobic dealings within the family would have to inhabit a wider space. Most people felt that the transfer worked, although there were a few gripes, of which more below.

Matt and the rest of the cast had taken it all extremely seriously. They had all got to know their subject matter, by learning about alcoholism and self-help groups, and although the subject matter was rather grim, this was an aspect of the job that Matt very much enjoyed. Adopting new personalities meant learning more about other areas, which played well with Matt's genuine curiosity about life. Because for all his earnestness, thoughtfulness and perception about the character he was playing, and despite that his appearance, his 'face with elbows', was striking, there was something slightly of the enthusiastic child about him. He retained this quality when it came to playing Doctor Who, another of the reasons it was such a success.

'I quite like the transitions of being an actor, because you get to explore these little pockets of life,' Matt said. 'So if you're playing a builder you get to know about building; if you're playing a scientist or a physician or something you get to know about physics. And similarly with this world, I like exploring their culture, that very sort of upper middle class, addictive ... that's part of the reason I love it.'

These investigations made him realise that the character of Henry was, in fact, a very complex one, far more so than it at first appeared. He might have been locked into a terrible and destructive relationship with his mother, but in a strange way it gave him something, too. 'At first, I couldn't get my head round it. I was like, why doesn't he [Henry] leave, why doesn't this character just leave?' he repeated in another interview. 'Because it's hell for him, obviously. But in fact it's not, it's hell and it's heaven at the same time. This is what's so difficult. This is why it's so interesting, because it's a complete contradiction. It's their relationship; it's like, actually she drives him mental, but he can't leave her because he's addicted to her and the love he gets off her, and the type of relationship they have. It's fascinating. So to understand it I've really had to look into that area of life.'

Only as an outsider, though. Although Matt worked very hard and was dedicated to his profession, there had never been any sign in his case of the insecurities so often found among actors, which could lead to any form of abuse, on his part. Rather, Matt sometimes seemed almost too normal to be an actor. He loved footie and going to music festivals. There was no inner darkness lurking inside. The close relationship with his parents was one element of that: they kept him grounded, even in those early days of beginning to feel his way as an actor, something that was to prove invaluable just a couple of years hence.

But the turmoil he had to experience on stage did take its toll, even when he had become used to performing it on stage every night. 'Me and Lindsay ... we did a run-through yesterday and we came out and even now we look dazed,' said Matt in the middle of rehearsals for the transfer to the West End. 'You have to take a deep breath, because you have to invest so much of your body and your heart and everything into it for it to work, you know, so it is tough, but I like it that way. Which was fortunate, for it was a necessary part of the whole process – but again, it spoke of great things to come one day.

The reviews for the new production were on the whole very positive, and quite a few of them singled out Matt for particular praise. They were also keen to emphasise that the subject matter, with its hints of incest even more shocking than the alcoholism and drug addiction, was very brave for everyone to tackle – writers, players and directors alike.

'Forget all the hype about Polly Stenham, at 21, being the youngest West End debutant since Christopher Hampton,' wrote Michael Billington in the *Guardian*, giving it four stars. 'What matters is that her 90-minute play, first seen at the Royal Court Theatre, has a quality of emotional desperation one more often associates with mature American dramatists like Tennessee Williams and Edward Albee than with cool young Brits. This is also one of the first English-language plays I can recall to deal explicitly with mother-son incest. Stenham's god-given gift ... is an ability to communicate pain and longing. The most moving aspect of the play is Martha's morbid fixation with her son. Lindsay Duncan brings to the role a blanched beauty and dreamy sensuality ... Duncan's brilliance is matched by Matt Smith whose hapless Henry is both one of those whom Oedipus wrecks and a residual snob, who greets his returning father with "you reek of duty-free".'

Simon Edge, in the *Daily Express*, also expressed his admiration, and agave it four stars. 'When Polly Stenham's Oedipal drama about a scarily dysfunctional upper-middle-class family was first performed at the Royal Court's tiny Upstairs theatre, the 20-year-old playwright was garlanded with "most promising" awards,' he wrote. 'Now the play has transferred to the West End, it is clear she deserved the acclaim. There are times when Jeremy Herrin's production seems underpowered. The comic part of the writing struggles to get through and some of the younger performers may be better suited to the original, smaller space. But that should not detract from the achievement of this intensely moving, skilfully crafted piece.'

Matt was singled out for praise by Charles Spencer in

the *Daily Telegraph*. 'When *That Face* opened at the Royal Court Theatre Upstairs in April 2007, I described it as one of the most astonishing dramatic debuts I had seen in more than 30 years of reviewing,' he wrote. 'Watching this West End transfer, the play seems every bit as fresh, passionate and blackly comic the second time around. Matt Smith is outstanding as the 18-year-old Henry, who is so pitiably desperate to save his mother from herself – his final scene of emotional collapse is shattering in its intensity.'

Matt also got a name check from Benedict Nightingale in *The Times*; he too gave the production four stars. '*That Face* ... has its prolix and its overstated moments, but it impressed everyone when it launched Stenham's career at the Royal Court's Theatre Upstairs last year,' he wrote. 'With reason too, since it catches the confusions of an *Ab Fab*-style family that's clearly been disintegrating since the father, Julian Wadham's Hugh, remarried and absconded to Hong Kong. Is it plausible that an 18-year-old would ditch his academic prospects to look after his awful mother explaining, "She's my life"? Well, Matt Smith has the emotional intensity to make you buy it. This gangling, gawky actor gives a performance to match the excellent Duncan.'

There was another four-star award from Nicholas de Jongh in the *Evening Standard*. '*That Face* ... generates such emotional power because it faces up unflinchingly to the consequences of a mother/son incestuous bond. This is the first play on the subject by an English author since Noel Coward's more oblique treatment in *The Vortex* ... Incest becomes the defining symptom of a rich, privileged, middle-class family in crisis and dysfunctional collapse. Although the dormitory incident beggars belief, betraying Stenham's immaturity, she handles the incest theme with assurance. In Jeremy Herrin's powerful, expressionistic production, a centre-stage bed is the single stage property. Here lies Henry's mother, Lindsay Duncan's Martha, a glazed alcoholic and blanched, petulant blonde, with something of several Tennessee Williams heroines about her. In spellbinding scenes that steer a wavering line between black comedy and a drama of erotic possessiveness ... Matt Smith's virtuoso performance makes it clear that Henry's life rather than Martha's has been ruined.'

Only Michael Coveney, in Whatsonstage.com was less impressed, giving it only three stars. 'It's an odd thing, transfers that don't quite live up to what all the fuss was about,' he wrote. 'Although Polly Stenham's first play *That Face* – a product of the Royal Court's Young Writers Programme, first seen in the Theatre Upstairs in April last year – is clearly the work of a fine new talent, it hasn't really hit the West End with a hurricane force. Jeremy Herrin's production has lost some of the engaging messiness it had Upstairs.'

Even so, it was clear a major new talent had arrived. Matt was clearly now set for great things, and the intensity of his performance meant that he displayed a range that was clearly going to serve him very well in the future. His Doctor had a comic edge, a lightness of touch, but *That Face* was as dark and destructive as it could be. Matt was obviously not just a one-trick pony: he was capable of far more, which, ultimately, would ensure a career once he stepped down as the Eleventh Doctor. Not that anyone wanted that to happen once he'd made the role his own.

With all this intensity going on in his professional life, Matt needed to find ways to relax, and had developed a wide array of interests outside the stage. He was a very musical person, a keen piano player, but also able with the flute and guitar as well. It gave him an outlet for all that boundless energy: 'What's nice about the music stuff is it's just a release, it's just something I enjoy,' he said. 'It's a way to do something else creative with my brain. You know, learn some lines, play the piano, learn some lines, play the piano. It works for me!'

He was a great fan of Radiohead, and felt that the rush he got from listening to them was something he wanted to recreate on stage. 'That's it,' he said. 'That's what I want when I go to the theatre, when I'm in a play, is them, and that experience that I get from them. I admire the musicianship; I admire the soul that goes into it, and the execution and the work, the preparation. Everything is done right, I think, and done with good intention and soul and heart and good spirit. They are a lesson to us all.'

In another interview, given after he'd landed the role of the Doctor, Matt went further still. 'They've been a real influence on my imaginative mind,' he said. 'I can muddle through "High and Dry" on the guitar, although I'm actually better on the piano. I asked for a piano in the Tardis but it hasn't happened. I'd love to see the Doctor rock up and play, but it'd have to be done in an inventive and silly way.'

Matt had a huge array of other interests, too. He loved poetry, especially (the now laureate) Carol Ann Duffy and he retained a passionate interest in football, albeit as a spectator rather than as a participant. 'Zinédine Zidane – the best player I've seen,' he enthused. 'He's grace, that man. Even, God love him, the head butt. It was a mistake, but by God he committed to it. Tony Adams was a player I really admired. Because he was clumsy like me? Yeah, perhaps. My best mate's dad would watch me play football and say, "I've got no idea how you can play football when you're that clumsy." It's always been a bit of a conundrum that I've got two feet that work. Stuart Pearce – my favourite footballer and a big influence. I remember that penalty, when he ran up to the fans after he scored. The last penalty he had taken, at the World Cup in 1990, he'd missed. I love my football, I really do.'

That was an understatement, if ever there was one. But importantly, he had come to accept that although it would remain a huge part of his life, it was not the be-all and end-all any more. It was clear now that his destiny was as an actor, taking on enormously challenging roles and making them his own. He could manage both the very serious and the deftly comic; he was prepared to take risks and expose his innermost emotions on stage. Most importantly, there was a complexity to his character, both on and off stage, which gave depth to his acting and allowed him to see the very different aspect of the individuals he played. And so now it was time for a very different role.

CHAPTER 9
PARTY ANIMALS

With the spectacular success of *That Face* behind him, Matt was now clearly ready to take part in a major television show. However, it wasn't to be quite the big breakthrough that everyone was expecting, and it certainly wasn't *Doctor Who*; rather, it was a BBC2 offering in 2007 called *Party Animals*. Purporting to be about the people of government, namely researchers, MPs and lobbyists, and concentrating on the lowlier individuals in the mêlée, it was a drama the critics liked but the viewers didn't. It never got more than one million viewers and a second series was not commissioned. But it did give Matt his first experience of making a television series, rather than a one-off appearance as he had done previously. And the role was nothing like as taxing as that from which he had just stepped down, which meant that body and soul, at least, were not to be tortured in quite the way they had been on stage.

It was never exactly clear why *Party Animals* never really took off. It followed in a fine tradition of shows about politics, of which the greatest is still *Yes Minister*, and the best more recently, *The Thick of It*. The subject matter – shenanigans in the corridors of power of both a personal and professional nature – provided plenty of scope for juicy plotlines, while its young cast was attractive and vigorous. Many felt that the real reason it didn't become a modern classic was that the BBC itself seemed pretty half-hearted about it. Yes, it had its own website, on which cast members, including Matt, were interviewed, but it was never really hyped up and as such, never really took off.

The set-up was as follows. Scott (Andrew Buchan) and Danny (Matt) Foster are the sons of an ex-Labour MP, and Danny is working as a researcher for the Home Office Junior Minister, Jo Porter (Raquel Cassidy). However, one crisis after another keeps hitting the Government, Jo's domestic life is in upheaval and Danny is forced to cope with all this, problems that are exacerbated by the arrival of a Machiavellian intern, Kirsty MacKenzie (Andrea Riseborough). Danny, 26, an intelligent but timid 'politics geek' who has not got as far as he should have by that stage, falls for Kirsty while at the same time trying to help a minister in decline.

Meanwhile, having made lots of contacts in government, his brother Scott has gone off to pursue a career in lobbying, a career that isn't going too well as the government is now in decline (the series was nothing if not topical). However, he has lunch with Ashika Chandiramani, who is the chief adviser to Shadow Minister James Northcote, who presents him with an opportunity; she herself is considering standing as an MP.

It certainly seemed to have potential when the series kicked off. According to the BBC website, 'Danny's a clever boy, an unashamed politics geek. And he's not without charm – he just lacks the confidence sometimes to really go for what he wants. Scott's always telling him to leave his current job as a researcher and get himself a better job with higher pay and more recognition. He's very capable. If only he'd believe in himself.

'Danny's been Jo's researcher since he left university and at 26 ought to have moved on by now. But he can't bring himself to leave her: he's also hoping that if he sticks with her long enough, when the promotions come she'll take him with her. Jo's difficult. At first Danny accepts this relationship without questioning – convincing himself it's part of his job description. But when the party whips start to notice Jo's decline, Danny realises he's going to have to take decisive action. But what will he do?'

At least Matt was used to playing a role involving a young man in thrall to an older woman, and he had clearly put as much thought into this role as he had the last. 'Danny has a romantic, moral take on the political

175

world and at the same time can be deeply cynical about life outside politics, his family etc,' he said. 'He has a dry sense of humour and a quick wit. Intellectually he's sharp and attentive; I suppose his brain is one of his most attractive features. Emotionally he's what you might deem uncultured; with women in particular Danny has an inability to express how he feels and be himself, at first. Underneath of course is a wry, sarcastic, witty, romantic waiting to knock a girl sideways and be the boyfriend of a lifetime! His timid nature romantically is of stark contrast to his persona at work where he can be dynamic, articulate and very productive.'

In other words, Danny was a world away from the sharp, lively, engaging Matt. Danny, one of life's underlings, was always hanging about in the background, trying and failing to do the right thing and not looking out for himself. Matt, meanwhile, was hugely popular with his fellow cast members, already proving himself highly accomplished in a number of wildly differing roles, and clearly set for great things. In fact, it's amazing in retrospect that anyone at all was surprised when he was named as the new Doctor Who.

But Danny was what Matt was concentrating on back then, and he had given some thought about what made Danny interested in politics. 'His opinions in general and of course his father,' he said. 'The death of his father, a person Danny was very close to, had an influence over his decision to enter politics. In doing so, however, Danny has developed his own political desire and drive. Academically he's always been a bit of book worm and what else would he do?'

Then there was the fact that Danny had not progressed in his career as much as he should have done. Why not? 'Loyalty to Jo and resolute belief in her ability. He could move because he's had offers,' said Matt. 'The great thing about Danny is despite his own emotional flaws regarding women, he's good at caring for people, being a shoulder or at some moments he's even a rock for others to lean on.'

He looked at other facets of Danny's character, as well.

'He's sensitive, yes, but not to an extreme,' he said. 'He's not wet so I don't think he's a prude by any means; he just knows what he likes in life. Drugs don't turn him on, work does. He works hard and should probably play harder but in not doing so has excelled in his academic career throughout his life.'

He was different from Matt in that respect, as well. Matt certainly worked hard, but he was not overly academic. (He was always rather embarrassed about the fact that his degree was a 2:2, although he cited, with some justification, the fact that for the last six months of his university career, he was actually on stage.) And he did retain some balance in his life. While he might not have pursued an actual career in football, it was still very important to him: he did not allow acting to become the be-all and end-all – apart from when it was really necessary, of course.

But he was very thorough when it came to analyzing the roles he played – he would be with Doctor Who, too. So then there was the relationship with his brother in the series. Was that important to him? 'Yes. Danny would be lost without Scott and vice versa,' said Matt (again, he was certainly becoming experienced at playing characters involved in complex familial relationships). 'Danny looks up to him in many ways; he is both inspired and repulsed by his brother. Danny, not being particularly close to his mother, feels an increased emotional connection to his brother and their unconditional love. Scott reminds Danny to have fun; he pushes Danny forward at work, as well as paying the rent.'

Did Matt think that Danny was living in the shadow of his father and brother? 'People may see it that way but not in Danny's mind,' he said. 'He's carrying forward a similar political nature to his father but not Scott – Danny doesn't want to be a lobbyist, wear those stupid, overpriced pointy shoes or sleep with the Tory candidate!'

As for Danny's feelings about Kirsty – 'He loves her, love is blind. She's pretty and she's quite funny. She treats him like shit, pays him little attention and uses him for her own personal gain quite ruthlessly. He doesn't know why but she rocks his world ... Kirsty respects Danny, his work ethic, his ability and his loyalty to her. He pays her too much attention and therein lies his flaw: he can't play hard to get or be sexy because he's too honest. He's an idiot for it but you love him as a result.'

When the series aired in 2007, it actually received pretty favourable reviews, another of the mysteries about why it never really took off. It was well plotted, well acted, went at a cracking place and could have been expected to do well. Had it done so, of course, it's possible that Matt might not have been chosen to play Doctor Who, given that Steven Moffat and co. wanted an unknown, and so in many ways it's as well for him that it didn't work out, but it was a disappointment at the time.

'The tone of *Party Animals* is pitched somewhere between *The Thick of It* and *This Life* and, surprisingly, they make a really nice job of it,' according to arieltelly.co.uk, and this was a view that was reflected across quite a number of reviewers. 'The central relationship between the brothers feels real despite the fact that they don't even look like they belong to the same species, never mind the same family. Raquel Cassidy plays the sussed but stressed party operator Jo excellently and Andrea Riseborough nails the dead-eyed porno stare of the ruthless careerist with chilling accuracy. It's tightly scripted with a great deal of care taken with the characters' motivation.'

Thecustardtv was one of the first to point out that the

cast was headed for greater things – and picked out Matt, in particular, as a standout cast member who would shortly be taking the world by storm. Just not in this series. 'An excellent cast. We expect thespian opulence from Colin Salmon and Raquel Cassidy (after *Lead Balloon*), but were somewhat surprised by the rich quality of the younger cast members – Andrew Buchan, Matt Smith, Shelley Conn and Andrea Riseborough – especially as we've seen little or nothing of them before ... Even though he was clumsily heralded as the 'hero' of the series through his admiration of the ANC and willingness to admit to his blunder that caused the collapse of Jo's (Raquel Cassidy) new ministerial policy, Danny was very likeable as he ineptly tried to woo the doe-eyed Machiavelli-in-sheep's-clothing Kirsty. Even his flaws were endearing, such as his witless efforts to slander Matt Baker by claiming that he got his position with slimy Tory shadow minister James Northcote through a blow job.'

Reviewers were not the only ones: Matt's co-stars in the series were in no doubt that he was headed for greater things. When it was announced that he was to be the new Doctor, Clemency Burton-Hill, who had starred alongside Matt in *Party Animals*, recalled her time acting with him with great enthusiasm. 'I remember sitting in a dingy rehearsal room reading through the script of the first episode and the rest of us being in stitches at Matt's character Danny, the fiercely principled Labour Party researcher who falls in love with a ruthless intern played by Andrea,' she wrote. 'Matt would often do the unexpected – a look or different inflection, perhaps – to make his character all the more fascinating. He is so enthusiastic about life. He was always raving about a quirky new band he had heard, and you would hear him whistling along the corridors before you saw him.'

It wasn't just critics who were watching the show with interest. So, too, were politicians, and the people who worked for them, who were rather bemused with the way they saw themselves pictured on screen. 'I objected to the cynicism of it all, and the way we were all portrayed as being so ruthless,' said Joshua Green, a researcher for the Liberal Democrats. 'Mind you, I do work for the Liberal Democrats. We don't drink that much or do all those class-A drugs either.'

Murad Ahmed, another Lib Dem researcher, saw something else they'd missed: 'Party Animals fails to capture my abiding memory of parliamentary life – the overwhelming boredom. And geeks, when bored, fall into a dangerous spiral of geekery. I remember fighting off another intern for the best part of an hour to sit at the researcher's desk when he wasn't in (it had the best view of the TV).'

Many were also very amused by the on-screen capering, although said that it was not all entirely true to life. 'It's actually very rare you'd get an MP sleeping with their own assistant – it's far more likely they'd be sleeping with someone else's,' said Alex Hilton, an erstwhile researcher to the MP Linda Perham. 'But there is some care taken to be discreet – you don't want to be known for the wrong kind of reputation. Parliament is rather like a cross between Hogwarts and a *Carry On* film. And it was quite a neat little place to stay overnight if you were out drinking in Soho. I remember one security guard who got very excited about a lady wandering around Portcullis House in a towel early one morning – she was a researcher for a Lib Dem MP. I certainly kipped over at least once or twice a month for the four years I was there – much safer than the night bus home. You can bumble back to Parliament, hazily show the security guard your clearance and collapse into your office. I used to keep a change of clothes there for that reason.'

As time went by, however, it began to become clear that the series wasn't taking off. No one seemed to be absolutely clear as to why this was the case – perhaps it was just too close to its brilliant predecessor, *The Thick of It*, and suffered by comparison. After all, *The Thick of It* actually aired a couple of decades after *Yes Minister*, and so although the similarities were there for all to see, there was a sufficient passage of time to ensure that the one wasn't always being judged against the other.

'The general consensus is that it's perfectly diverting, but not quite *The Thick of It*,' wrote Martin Bright, political editor for the *New Statesman*. 'But then perhaps if the programme makers had intended it to be *The Thick of It*, they would not have called it *Party Animals* but something else. *The Thick of It*, perhaps. As the programme's political consultant I can confirm that every inaccuracy in the programme was identified in advance by me and ignored by the programme makers for artistic reasons.'

But it did have something – hence the general feeling of puzzlement when it didn't quite take off. One anonymous blogger on the *Guardian* website's Comment is Free pages was well qualified to judge: he (or she) worked for the Labour Party. 'I liked it. I didn't mean to, but I did,' he began. 'There is plenty wrong. Firstly, the actors are all better looking. And the policy stuff is rubbish. MPs' researchers do not write Government policy, much as they wish they could. Do researchers swipe documents left by the opposition in the loo? Sure. But the only notes I've ever picked up in a Westminster toilet had nothing more significant on them than someone else's piss. So what have they got right? Well, the offices look like Portcullis (though there are no gruesome portraits of David Cameron in the real corridors). Most of all, they've captured the reason we're all here: everyone in Westminster village is either addicted to or dealing in gossip, hope, and power.' In other words, powerful stuff, that should have, but didn't, quite make a really classic TV drama.

The few viewers it did get were on the whole very enthusiastic about it. Indeed, there was a good deal of online debate about why it hadn't taken off more than it did. That previously mentioned lacklustre behaviour on the part of the BBC seemed to have something to do with it: the channel had just never really got behind the new show enough to make it work.

'It's really bizarre...why would BBC commission a series, and then not bother to promote it?' was one typical blog, from Mayogirl on Digitalspy. 'Where's the sense in that? Actually, what the Beeb did here, was even worse than that – they put it on against their own fairly popular drama on BBC1 (*New Street Law*) and also on a night when there was lots of Champions League football, Carling Cup semi-final, Jamie Oliver etc etc ... its opening rating was 1.3 million, and at its peak, episode 7, it reached 1.4 million. It was on too early, and on BBC2, and basically the towel was thrown in by episode 2 in terms of promotion. At 8 episodes, there wasn't an awful lot of time for people to get attuned to it, especially as there was a fair bit of setting the scene, and introducing the characters in the first two episodes It's a terrible pity, because it really was that good ... very well written, acting – absolutely top drawer (I have no doubt that all of these young actors will go on to good things). brilliant soundtrack, beautifully shot ... everything about this programme was class. It took some heavy criticism after the first couple of episodes, but I think most of the critics were won over in the end.'

Even though the series did not make a big splash with the viewers, it still promised great things for all involved, however, and a year later, when it was confirmed that another series was not to be commissioned, the talented young cast were all assured they had big futures. 'Scott, Danny, Ashika and Kirsty were the young political researchers grappling with messy personal lives in last year's drama *Party Animals*,' said the *Observer*. 'The BBC2 series developed a cult following but never drew more than a million viewers and was not re-commissioned. But if it did not prove the hit BBC executives had hoped, it gave the actors a platform for success. Here's how its cast of relative unknowns went from Westminster lackeys to West End and television stars.' And so a round-up ensued, including Matt, although there was no mention of the Doctor or the Tardis. That was, as yet, still very much in the future.

And that was all very much the highlights of Matt's career until the Doctor showed up, as he was shortly to do. He was making a big name for himself, proving popular with his peers and was on the cusp of getting the role that would turn him into a household name. It was 2008, David Tennant was beginning to think beyond the confines of the Tardis and Matt was shortly to land the biggest role of his career.

But he wasn't the only one about to stage a huge breakthrough. The Doctor had to have a companion, and in order for it to work, there had to be a huge amount of chemistry between the Doctor and that companion. So just who was the next Doctor's assistant to be?

CHAPTER 10

WHO'S THAT GIRL?

Nothing could match the furore surrounding the search for a new Doctor Who. But there is also always a great deal of interest in the Doctor's assistant, almost invariably an attractive young woman whose role has been that of helpmeet, admirer and, if truth be told, someone for the fathers to ogle at when the family watches the show. While they have never been passive, the Doctor's assistants did often appear to be there in order to be rescued by the Doctor in the earlier manifestations of the show – but these days they are showing themselves to be adventurers in their own right.

The prototype for the new style of assistant was, of course, Rose Tyler, so memorably played by Billie Piper, who set the bar very high for her successors. And none of them in the days of David Tennant – with the possible exception of Bernard Cribbins, who was also a companion of sorts – quite made the impact she did. But when it was the turn of the Eleventh Doctor to enter the Tardis, the show's producers wanted to make sure they got a memorable assistant who was more than a match for the Doctor.

And so it was to prove. The Eleventh Doctor's assistant, Amy Pond, was popular right from the start. Introduced as a little girl, the first to see the Doctor's latest incarnation, and transformed shortly afterwards into a young woman, Amy is played by Karen Gillan. She sounded quite as overwhelmed as Matt when she, too, discovered she would be travelling in time and space: 'I am absolutely over the moon,' she said. 'The show is such a massive phenomenon that I can't quite believe I'm going to be a part of it.' A controversial part, too – Karen's legs were long, and her skirts were going to be short. Her profession was as a kissogram, the first ever in that interesting line of work to take the worries of the universe, along with the Doctor, on her shoulders. But these were enlightened times.

Everyone who becomes involved in *Doctor Who* sounds a little overwhelmed when talking about it – even Christopher Eccleston – and Karen was no exception. As with Matt, initial negotiations had been cloaked in secrecy, so much so that it was almost a surprise to learn that Karen herself knew she was up for the role. Not that she had been told a great deal more. 'I knew that the audition was for the part of the Companion, but I wasn't allowed to tell anyone about it,' she said. 'They even had a code name for the role because it was so top secret. The code name was "Panic Moon", an anagram of Companion, which I thought was really clever. It was one of the strangest experiences ever; it was a really weird feeling. I found out on the day of my second audition with Matt [Smith], so at least I didn't have a really long wait. It just didn't feel real, and I couldn't believe it!' It was, however, to be quite a while before she could tell anyone else her news.

When the announcement did come out, Amy was given a hearty endorsement by the people who mattered. Steven Moffat was delighted that she was on board. 'We saw some amazing actresses for this part, but when Karen came through the door the game was up,' he said. 'Funny, and clever, and gorgeous, and sexy. Or Scottish, which is the quick way of saying it. A generation of little girls will want to be her. And a generation of little boys will want them to be her too.' That was something of an understatement. Most of the Doctor's assistants ended up as pinups – Tardis totty, if you like – but Amy was to become an out-and-out sex symbol, acquiring an army of fans in her own right.

The trick of having two Amys, the much younger one, and the 20-something to introduce viewers to the new Doctor, brought about another happy coincidence. The infant Amy was played by Karen's cousin Caitlin Blackwood, also an actress with quite a future ahead. But although they were cousins, they had never actually met before the episode was filmed. 'Caitlin was born and grew up in Northern Ireland and Karen grew up in Scotland,' said Caitlin's mother Linda. 'So they actually only met for the first time at the read-through on set. It was an emotional moment. People kept commenting that they were so alike.'

Caitlin herself was thrilled with the experience. 'It was scary seeing myself up on the screen for the first time,' she said. 'I loved getting to know Karen and chatting with her. I got to meet some Daleks and went inside the Tardis too.'

But despite the relationship, there were no favours. Karen related that Caitlin had had to go through the audition process just like everyone else, and that she, Karen, had had nothing to do with Caitlin's selection. But she, too, was delighted by the choice of the actress to play little Amy. 'We didn't have many scenes together, but we saw each other around set, and that was nice,' she said.

And so who is the lithe redhead, who gives the Doctor as good as he gets and has so intrigued male fans of the show? Karen is a Scottish actress, born 28 November 1987 in Inverness. Certainly, nothing in her background hinted at the glories that were to lie ahead. Karen's father, Raymond John, was a Day Centre Manager, her mother, Marie, a housewife. She was as little known as Matt when she was appointed to the role, something the producers clearly wanted to use to their advantage: since both were a totally unknown quantity, no one had the faintest idea what to expect, a fact that helped both of them to come to terms with what was happening to them. Both were getting drawn into the *Doctor Who* frenzy: as soon as it was announced that they had got the two plum roles, there was intensive speculation as to how they'd carry it off, to say nothing of how they were going to play the part. It isn't easy even for seasoned performers to cope with the attention that goes with such a high-profile show, but to go from total unknown to player in one of the biggest cultural phenomena in the country, is a challenge. Total unknown to immersion in the full glare of publicity. That's quite a leap for anyone to have to make.

'That's one of the lovely things about working with Matt because we are going through this crazy experience together,' said Karen in an interview after filming had begun. 'I'm sure it would be very different if he was already an established Doctor and then I came into it, but it's just so nice to share this journey with someone who's going through the same thing as you. It's really exciting times because there's a whole new turnover in a way, so it's new and exciting and fresh. Having worked with him for the last nine months, I find it weird to think that anyone else played the Doctor. He's completely taken on the role and made it his own.'

Matt himself had been effusive about Karen, calling her beautiful and talented. She went on to repay the compliment in full. The producers had seen that he had that crucial certain something to take on the role, and Karen testified to it, as well. For all his youth, he somehow managed to exude the wisdom of centuries. And although he was actually only a few years older than Karen, it was quite possible for the viewer to believe that a few centuries separated them, too. Karen certainly saw that he had the character and magnetism to make something of the role. 'You know what? When Matt walks into a room, you know that he's there,' she said. 'He's got that aura about him and that's what makes him so brilliant at playing the Doctor because his Doctor is a force of nature. He's very eccentric and playful and funny and we have a great time together filming.' This was a very big clue as to how his Doctor was going to come across on screen, too.

Karen's appointment also maintained the Scottish link with the show. David Tennant had been a Scot, but he had played the role as English (Russell T Davies had been heard to comment that he wasn't going to turn *Doctor Who* into a tour of provincial accents), whereas Karen was very much going to stick to her roots. 'She will be Scottish, yes,' she said. 'In my first audition, I did it in an

English accent and in my own accent. It was up in the air in the beginning, but then we decided to go with my own accent, which is nice.'

It was a huge break at a young age, but something Karen had been striving for, for most of her life. Karen knew she wanted to try her hand as an actress from very early on. When she was 16, she enrolled at Edinburgh's Telford College; after that she moved on to the prestigious Italia Conti Academy of Theatre Arts in London to take a BA (Hons) acting degree. But she had had a normal childhood, just like anyone else. 'I got teased for being a redhead when I was younger, which is strange because I'm Scottish and there are loads of us – we should unite forces!' she said. 'I love my red hair. When I was 15, I dyed half my hair pink, inspired by the "Bootylicious" video. My parents went mental! I had it for a good few months – I kept re-dyeing it, because I thought it looked really cool. That's my biggest fashion faux pas to date...'

She was lucky. Had there been other such sartorial mistakes, they would almost certainly have turned up. As it was, however, Karen had the face and body of a model, which she had indeed been in the past, and so after the *Doctor Who* announcement was made, she posed in various photo shoots looking extremely glamorous. The fathers were clearly in for a treat. Karen's comments about her hair were apposite. Indeed, the BBC was no doubt delighted in having a red-haired assistant on board the Tardis. When Matt Smith first regenerated, and was attempting to come to terms with his new appearance, he commented, 'I'm still not ginger,' eliciting complaints from 143 viewers. One mother in particular was livid: 'I think it is totally inappropriate for the Doctor to make fun of people with ginger hair,' she snapped. 'It is a programme children watch, and I think it will encourage bullying.' Now, at least, the Beeb could point out that there was, in fact, a ginger inhabitant of the Tardis. 'We've received complaints from viewers who believed a line in *Doctor Who: The End of Time* was insulting to people with ginger hair,' said a spokesperson. 'We would like to reassure viewers that Doctor Who doesn't have an anti-ginger agenda whatsoever. This was a reprise of the line in the "Christmas Invasion" episode in 2005, when David Tennant discovers that he's not ginger, and here he is, missing out again – disappointed he's still not ginger.'

Well, Karen was, and proud of it. Nor was it exactly holding her back. Upon leaving the Italia Conti Academy, she had started to get some acting experience, too. Karen had appeared in an episode of *Rebus*, 'A Question Of Blood', in 2006, playing a character called Terry Cotter, and in the television hospital drama *Harley Street*. She was also part of the ensemble cast in *The Kevin Bishop Show*, a comedy sketch series, in which she did impersonations of celebrities such as Katy Perry and Angelina Jolie, as well as playing very many different characters. It was the television equivalent of repertory theatre: a very good training in that you had to learn to play lots of different parts.

However, after that initial burst, work dried up, and for a time, at least, it seemed as though her acting career might be at an end. As is so often the way with setbacks, this was ultimately to work to her advantage – and there can be few members of the acting profession who haven't had their fair share of times when they were 'resting' – but it was very difficult to cope with at the time. By now based in London, Amy went to work in The Pilgrim pub in London's Kennington, not at all the future she had been planning for herself. 'It was depressing, not working for so long,' she said. 'I hated not being involved in acting, but looking back on it, I'm pleased it happened. Otherwise I wouldn't know what it's like to have a normal job.'

What rescued her was not acting, but modelling – at 5ft 11, she was the right height, and as *Doctor Who* fans were to discover, had very long legs that were perfect for a spell on the catwalk. First Karen was approached to be a model for Allegra Hicks during the 2007 London Fashion Week for the autumn/winter catwalk show. She then worked as a model for the launch party of Nicola Roberts' (from girl band Girls Aloud) Dainty Doll make-up range; this was, in fact, caught on film in the course of Nicola's episode of the documentary *The Passions of*

Girls Aloud. Had her acting career not been suddenly resurrected, there's every chance she would have made it as a successful model instead.

However, *Doctor Who* came up and it very soon became obvious that Karen was the woman for the role. 'Then I got the recall, the second audition,' she told one interviewer. 'That was when I started sweating. This huge thing. And it was so secretive I couldn't even tell BBC reception where I was going. I had to pretend it was for something called *Panic Moon*.' It later turned out that she was actually the last actress to audition for the role – although it was clear she was the correct choice right from the start.

In some ways, Karen was more Christopher Eccleston than Matt Smith when it came to the part, in that she had not been a diehard fan of *Doctor Who*. But she was well aware how important it was in terms of popular culture. 'To be honest, I wasn't really a huge follower of *Doctor Who* before I got this part,' she said. 'I mean I knew it was huge, but … I was nothing like my mum, who's a proper diehard Whovian. She's got a Tardis moneybag, and Dalek bubble-bath. But having read the first episode I was utterly smitten, and with the character. Amy's a sassy lady, funny and passionate, and her relationship with the doctor has a really interesting dynamic.'

It was known from the start that the Doctor and Amy were to share a kiss: did this imply they were in love?

Karen had very much her own take on it all. 'She has a love for him, a really deep love for him,' she said. 'But not romantic. It's been an education in itself to work with Matt, who's so endlessly inventive, bringing something new to it every day rather than falling into the easy default scared face. That's one of the challenges; you're faced with life-threatening situations every episode, but you can't just widen your eyes all the time. Yes, this doctor is preeeetty good.'

And then there was the matter of the wardrobe, on which Amy had also had some input. Having done some modelling, she was well aware of the impact of appearance, and those very short skirts were in part down to her. 'She [Amy] gets to wear all these small skirts, which I will admit was very cold, but also very cool,' she said. 'They originally wanted to put me in trousers, but I did say I'd like to wear a skirt because – you'll understand when you watch it. Actually I think I love Amy. I'm in love with her. I want to be her.'

And so Amy began to prepare for the challenges ahead. It was a challenge, too. Matt might have been taking on the central role, but it was vitally important to get the chemistry right between him and his assistant, on top of which, Amy had to be able to compare well to her predecessors. It was not going to be an easy task.

Karen knew it, too. 'It's a pretty terrifying role, but a huge privilege to be part of an iconic show,' she said, sounding very much like her new co-star. 'I'm following a long line of great actresses who have played the companion, so it's quite daunting. I'd love to sit down with them and have a good chat about it.' Karen, like Matt, knew that there was a long journey ahead.

CHAPTER 11

THE DOCTOR'S ASSISTANT

But each assistant had to find her own way into the role. And like Matt, Karen lived in a world where everything was instant and immediate. As soon as the new series started to air, the bloggers would be sharing their views; even before the show began, she couldn't go anywhere without people noticing. It was all very scary and new.

But it was uncanny how much her experiences mirrored Matt's. Just as he had had to keep his big secret after being appointed to the role, so Amy, too, was not able to tell the world about this plum role that had landed on her lap. Unlike Matt, though, she couldn't tell her parents, because she thought the weight of the knowledge would just be too great. 'My boyfriend knew, but I didn't tell anyone else, including my mum – she's a huge *Doctor Who* fan and I didn't want to lumber her with the secret,'

Karen said. 'I only told her an hour before the public found out. I couldn't tell my mum because she's such a Whovian. I knew if I told her she was just going to burst with excitement, so I thought a nicer way to do it would be to tell her just before it was publicly announced. It was absolutely agonising! I had my phone in my hand and I really wanted to tell her, because I could tell my immediate family and that was all, but I opted out of that. I think that was for the best.'

As a matter of fact, the role of Amy Pond was not Karen's first appearance in *Doctor Who*. That had come in the David Tennant days, when the relevant companion was Catherine Tate, and when Karen appeared as a Roman soothsayer in an episode called 'The Fires Of Pompeii'. It was becoming something of a tradition for Doctor Who's companions to have appeared in a previous episode – Freema Agyeman auditioned for several parts, and played the role of Adeola Oshodi in 'Army of Ghosts' before she, too, became a companion – and indeed, the series had a regular troop of artistes who would appear more than once. And like the others, Karen's initial appearance had been very different from the role she was eventually to assume. Indeed, she was unrecognisable. And Karen had very happy memories of her first venture into the show. 'That was so much fun and just knowing how excited my mum was about that made me think that, definitely, I wasn't going to tell her about my next role!' she said.

And the next role, of course, was going to be far more high profile. The fact that Amy had appeared before meant that she had had a very minor insight into what she was getting into. No one had heard of Matt Smith back then (it was 2008) and Karen could not have conceived that she would shortly herself be one of the show's biggest stars. She was keen to emphasise, however, that that earlier appearance had nothing to do with her getting the role of Amy Pond.

'But it's not linked to me getting the companion role in any way because it's a brand new team for this series,' she explained. 'I suppose it couldn't have hurt to have already been in the *Doctor Who* environment and to know what was involved, but they are just completely different characters so it requires a completely different approach.'

As time went on, Amy began to experience quite what it was like to be part of the whole *Doctor Who* set-up. The actors who play Doctor Who himself are warned about what it will be like, but it's not until they actually experience it that the reality sinks in. The same applies for his assistant, as Karen was beginning to learn. 'It's a role like no other,' she said. 'When you get involved with *Doctor Who*, it's not just filming the show, there's so much that goes with it. It's lovely that people are so interested in the show and are really passionate about it. When I first got the role, I was really tempted to go on the internet, but I don't think that's the best idea. It's quite strange to have people forming these opinions of you and they haven't seen you yet. I thought it was best I ignored all that and just concentrated on the acting.'

Like Matt, she was charged with absolute secrecy about what they would all be getting up to once the show began – and like Matt she couldn't speak more highly about what was in store. 'I can't say too much – because I want you all to watch it – but Steven Moffat has created such a brilliant companion character,' she told a crowd of journalists. 'She's completely relevant to the storyline and she's a very sassy young lady and certainly very questioning of the Doctor and not in awe of him all the time. She takes him on and gives him a run for his money. There's an interesting dynamic between Amy and the Doctor, which is due to the way they meet.'

As with all the best companions, especially Rose, Amy was also not going to stand for any nonsense from her companion in the Tardis. 'The Doctor is definitely an alpha male and Amy is an alpha female, so when they meet, they combust,' she said. 'She's very sassy and feisty and gives the Doctor a run for his money. They have quite a turbulent relationship but it's also really passionate and they care about each other. I think Amy is quite similar to the Doctor and feels quite alone.'

Karen and Matt, meanwhile, were getting on so well that they were able to tease one another increasingly in public. He had called her completely mad; Karen responded by commenting on something that a lot of people had been commenting on – the shape of Matt's head. 'I've never seen anything like it,' she said. 'And he has an aura as well. A head and an aura. He has some strange mannerisms but he really doesn't see it. All those odd things he does with his hands. As you spend more time with Matt you don't notice it so much and he becomes normal. And that's how it must be for him. He feels normal. But he isn't. Which is great for the Doctor.'

This of course spilled into the screen relationship. 'Sometimes they're like brother and sister, getting at each other and winding each other up,' Karen continued. 'But Amy is also attracted to the Doctor. It's just that she's not attracted to him in a romantic way. That's what separates her from the other companions who came before. She's not secretly in love with the Doctor. She wants something else.'

The chemistry between them was perfect, and that was a result of the off-screen relationship, too. 'We just kind of bounce off each other,' said Karen. 'The banter that you see on screen – that's what we're like all day on set. I sometimes wonder if it's our way of keeping our energy up between scenes, but it's all subconscious. And I think we might have been like that if we'd met in any other situation. The one thing I never wanted to do with Amy was to base her on any kind of formula, to conform to what works – or what has worked – in a companion; you know, the whole, likeable, girl-next-door business. Amy is likeable, I hope, but she's not ordinary. She's quite complicated and there are layers to explore. So I was taking a few risks with her and I think it works.'

Along with all the attention, Karen was also having to get used to the other, faintly surreal aspects of her new role. For a start, she was beginning to see herself everywhere – not just in photographs but in all the merchandising that went along with every new *Doctor Who*. 'The other day I was looking at a version of myself in a new computer game and I asked for the legs to be changed,' she confided to one interviewer, saying they were 'almost like a body-builder's'. Those legs, of course, were becoming famous in their own right, as Amy's unique calling card.

Karen was also beginning to feel the total immersion that so many have experienced when they started working on the show. 'We work such long hours that it completely dominates your life,' she said. 'I had a few days off once and I didn't like it when I came back because I felt out of touch. I was out of it for two days and I felt I'd lost Amy. She's a lot cooler than me. She has a different walk from me. She struts. She's bad. It saddens me to think of the day when it'll all be over. But once you're in *Doctor Who* you're in it forever.' You could say that again.

As interest grew in Karen, attention also focused on her

private life. She had a boyfriend, the 24-year-old photographer Patrick Green, who, she said, was perfectly relaxed about her near clinches with the Doctor. The two were snapped out and about, on one occasion at the Bonsai Tree Farm in Suffolk – Bonsai is Patrick's hobby. He, too, was beginning to learn what it was like to be involved with such a popular television show, albeit one removed. But from now on, there would be almost as much interest in him as there was in Karen. He certainly seemed able to take it on.

When the debut aired, Patrick returned with Karen to the family home in Inverness to watch the show. The family, of course, were beside themselves. Marie, Karen's mother, could not have been more proud: 'It's absolutely fantastic,' she said. 'I'm a Whovian and proud of it. I've been a fan for years. From even before Karen got a part in 2008 in the episode "The Fires of Pompeii". I didn't even dare dream then that this could ever happen. Now I have to pinch myself to remind me it really is true. She really is Doctor Who's assistant.'

A further sign of Karen's popularity came via a website called the Redheaded Goddess Forums, dedicated to the world's most attractive redheads. Pictures of her surfaced looking a little the worse for wear as she came out of a nightclub; these just made the viewers fancy her even more.

'She's quite mesmerizing,' posted one.

'She's pretty cute,' posted another. 'She has what I would call a "sweet" face. I reckon babies would smile at her.'

'Karen's been an overnight sensation and has become the most popular redhead on the site,' said a spokesman. 'I didn't even know who she was until one of our members posted about her on my forum. The forum received thousands of hits on the Karen Gillan thread, so much so that I thought it was under some kind of hacker attack. There's a lot of chat on the site about her now and Karen's star really seems to be rising here. It's safe to say there's been a huge following on the site since *Doctor Who* started. The pictures have helped.'

But she was more than that, too. Karen new that however successful she was in the role, her time on *Doctor Who* was finite, as it was with everyone, and so she had to plan ahead. And so she had been looking at other avenues to explore, too. Coincidentally, just before she was cast as Amy Pond, Karen landed a role in a low budget film called *Outcast*, starring James Nesbitt and Kate Dickie, and from the start, it was clear that for the more conservative fans, this role would come as something of a shock.

Despite the fact that Amy was a kissogram with a proclivity for very short skirts and a tendency to make passes at the Doctor, there was still a very wholesome quality about her, something singularly lacking in her role in *Outcast*. It was a, 'B-movie mixture of nudity and violence,' said an insider on the film, adding, 'The BBC would never have let Karen make it now that she's famous for being Amy.' It was to be premiered at the Edinburgh International Film Festival, and was also set in Edinburgh, in which Nesbitt chases his ex-lover (on film) Dickie into a council estate where a killer is on the loose. Terror ensues.

It was a very different kind of monster from the ones that Karen spent her time grappling with on the set of *Doctor Who*. But for however long she was to play the role of Amy, Karen had indubitably made her mark. She, too, was now a part of the long and ongoing history of *Doctor Who*.

CHAPTER 12

THE DOCTOR AND THE WOMEN

In recent years, it has been a given that the new Doctor who will be a heartthrob. In the earliest days of the programme, the Doctors tended to be more grandfathers than Romeos, but as the Doctors have got younger, so their appeal has increased. And certainly since Christopher Eccleston helped to revive the series in 2005, the new Doctor can be sure of a fair bit of female attention, as David Tennant was to discover. In his case, his fan club certainly contained more than a few adoring women – of all ages, not just teens.

And so it was with Matt Smith. But the actors who play the Doctor have private lives, too. Alongside the adoring fans, Matt had quietly had a series of girlfriends, the first of whom he met in slightly unusual circumstances. When he was told that he'd got the role of the Eleventh Doctor, and was going to have to be prepared to be recognised in supermarkets, he revealed that that was exactly where he'd met his first real love. 'I haven't had to cross that bridge yet because I am not as publically recognisable as I will be in a few months so I don't know exactly what it will be like,' he said. 'I hope I will be able to sort the wheat from the chaff if you meet someone at Tesco or whatever. And you never know. I met my first girlfriend at Tesco walking down the meat aisle with my dad. A loving relationship is important and rewarding, and I am a romantic.'

Like any man of his age, Matt had had the odd fling – including one with Billie Piper, if some reports were to be believed, but at the time he learned that he'd got the role, he revealed that he had a girlfriend he'd met in Brazil, but that, 'It's a nightmare because she's 6,000 miles away.' He wouldn't say who the lucky girl was, but it wasn't long before she was named as Mayana Moura, a singer who divided her time between Rio and New York, and who in fact bore an uncanny resemblance to Matt. The two had met when Matt was on holiday in Rio; he'd extended his allotted time there from two weeks to six and they had taken it from there.

'Mayana and Matt were introduced to each other last January at the fashionable Rio nightspot Club 00,' said Bruno Astuto, a Brazilian society columnist who knew Mayana in February 2009. 'Matt went back to England and they kept in touch. He was so in love that he came to

Brazil a second time and they started to seriously date. Then Mayana went to England to see him. She has been over three times in all. He was introduced to her family and last month, during his latest visit to Rio, they began talking about marriage. It would be a great match. They have been together for one year. They celebrated on New Year's Eve when they joined a group of friends for a party in a penthouse overlooking the beach in Copacabana.'

Mayana, a very striking looking woman with green eyes and long flowing hair, was born in Rio on 19 August 1982, and started out as a model after being spotted by the famous photographer Mario Testino. Because of him, she appeared in a magazine fashion shoot under the headline, 'The New Girl From Ipamena', and went on to spend some time in Paris, appearing for Karl Lagerfeld in Chanel. She then moved into music and acting, founding a punk band called Glass and Glue with the Brazilian stylist Marina Franco, and getting an agent in the process. But the fact that she, like Matt, was on the brink of a career breakthrough on the other side of the world did not bode well.

'Matt wants Mayana to move to England but she is really involved in this band project and she does not want to disappoint her band mate Marina,' said Bruno Astuto. 'She and Matt are both very young, they are both at the start of brilliant careers and they are in love. I just don't know how it will end. It is a real dilemma.'

Alas, it was, and one that was not to end happily. A long-distance relationship is difficult enough in itself to maintain, but as soon as it was announced that Matt was to enter the Tardis, not only was attention focused on him in a way that it never had been before, but it meant that his schedule was so busy he hardly had time to think. And so in the summer of 2009 came the first of the reports that they'd split, although it was not properly confirmed until the following year. 'Matt and Mayana adore each other, but the timing was not right and the relationship just ran its course,' said a friend. 'Matt has been up in Cardiff for the past few weeks filming and he will be in Wales for the next four months on a very gruelling shoot. This job means the world to him.'

Initially, it seemed that Matt was planning on devoting all his energy to his new job. After all, it was utterly consuming at times, very long days for months on end, and an opportunity of the kind that comes along once in a lifetime. Work was to be his priority and nothing else. 'I am afraid I won't be one of those celebrities falling out of nightclubs with girls on my arm,' he said, a tad portentously. 'I don't have the time. We're filming seven or eight months of the year. Work is my mistress ... Most of the fans I've met have been very kind and very generous. But there is one mad one who keeps comparing me to a hedgehog.'

Then there was the minor matter of his co-star. Karen

Gillan was an extremely good-looking woman, according to some the Doctor's sexiest assistant ever, not least Matt himself, and it wasn't unprecedented for a Doctor to have a relationship with a companion. Tom Baker had married one of his, after all. But both were adamant that this was not the case. 'I've got a boyfriend and we've been together for four years,' Karen protested. 'Matt is a good-looking guy, but he's like my older brother.'

Matt himself was also keen to dampen that particular line of speculation. 'She's a beautiful woman, you know, but we work together,' he said. 'That would be an error. She's my mate, Kaz. I just take the mick out of her everyday. She is as mad as a box of cats – in a brilliant way. We're both pretty mad, I think.' And they were both involved with other people. But they were young, attractive and constantly in one another's company, while on-set romances are a notorious feature of the show business world. It was just that in this case, there was nothing to say.

Of course, a great deal of this occurred because there was speculation about whether this would be the first time that the Doctor (the character, not the actor) was officially romancing his assistant. The series had not yet started to air, but already there were rumours doing the rounds about the scene in which Amy propositions him, making it inevitable that speculation would spill over into real life. Amy was certainly racier than the other assistants: how would to Doctor be able to resist?

'The truth is, old *Doctor Who* was an entirely sexless series,' said Steven Moffat. 'The Doctor wasn't the only sexless character among a whole lot of sexually motivated ones. The Brigadier never got a date either, and no one bothered to mention it – neither did Sarah Jane Smith. It was that kind of show, as a lot of shows were in those days. When *Doctor Who* came back, it had to fit into modern television. The question is: would a young girl hanging out with this older, dangerously attractive, mad, charming, brilliant man, maybe now and then notice? She would. That's human nature. Are we really supposed to be believe back in the day that Tegan never had a look at the Doctor, even when he was Peter Davison? That Sarah Jane Smith never thought about that charismatic, older Tom Baker as being really not bad? It would happen. You have to address it, and you can't ignore it. I would say of the old show that there's always that sort of latent romance going on. It's never expressed, but when Jon Pertwee says goodbye to Jo Grant, he doesn't look too pleased about it. He doesn't look too pleased that she's run off with someone she haplessly describes as a younger version of him. He's clearly cheesed off and it's not the reaction of a proud parent. So the element is there, but as to how we do it this time, that is really centrally and importantly part of the story of this series – so it's unwise to tell a story before you start.'

For all the hints that the two find each other attractive on some level, however, everyone involved realised that it would destroy the dramatic tension if the Doctor and Amy really did become an item. Matt certainly thought so. 'There is always room for romance in *Doctor Who* but to be honest, the idea of the companion and the Doctor getting together is a bit of a tired story by now,' he said. 'There is only so far it can go. What happens? So, they get together, travel around the universe, end of story? There has to be more to it than that. It has to be about adventure, magic and exploration. Those are the things we're interested in this season, really.'

There was another reason the Doctor couldn't find love – he simply didn't have the time. 'It's because he's too busy,' he said. 'He finds humans fascinating but imagine if you'd travelled round for 900-plus years on your own with this great weight behind you. He's an addict – if he stopped saving the world he'd be in real trouble.' He was also 'an intergalactic genius, a superhero-ish mad, fumbling, bumbling, science geek.'

In truth, though, both Matt and Karen couldn't help teasing us about what had gone on between their two characters. There had been that kiss in Amy's bedroom – 'Matt is a superb kisser,' said Karen innocently. 'We had to do quite a few takes and there was quite a bit of giggling. Thankfully the kissing scene wasn't the first scene we had to do because that would have been weird. We were well into the run of the series when it came up so we'd gotten to know one another really well.'

'Those luscious lips!' said Matt, not to be outdone. 'I'd rate her a nine, stroke 10, for kissing. How can anyone not love Kaz?'

Despite his own protestations, however, it really didn't look as if he was going to be single for long. Fans were throwing themselves at him and he had suddenly become a very interesting proposition for the type of woman who wanted to go out with the hottest new woman on the scene. Matt didn't seem to have trouble attracting girlfriends, but even if he had, his new status meant that there would be girls who wanted to be with him queuing up round the block. He might not have quite made it to David Tennant-style heartthrob status (yet), but there was no question that he now had the pick of the bunch.

And for all Matt's protestations that he was wedded to his work and that the Doctor was a far more important figure in his life than any woman could be, it soon became apparent that it was just conceivably possible that he might have got his eye on someone after all. If truth be told, it would have been strange if he had not. Matt was a healthy, red-blooded young man, who had just come out of a relationship with a very beautiful Brazilian woman, and he was almost bound to be looking for someone else.

In fact, initially the story came out as just a hint. A journalist asked him if he was still seeing Mayana: 'No, no, no, no,' was the reply. In that case, what exactly was Matt looking for in a woman? 'Oh gosh! Daisy Lowe is taken, so that's out of the question. Ha ha! ... She's a pretty lady ... Oh, I don't know. Someone lovely with a good heart who enjoys the things I enjoy ... who plays the guitar.'

Daisy Lowe was indeed taken, but matters change all the time, especially when you are very young and it involves affairs of the heart. And so it was that at around the time that Matt's first *Doctor Who* series started airing, he found himself with a new, very high-profile girlfriend. Was it love? Would it last? Who, exactly, was this Daisy Lowe who had won his heart?

CHAPTER 13

FRESH AS
A DAISY

D aisy Lowe is second-generation show business. Born
27 January 1989, her mother is Pearl Lowe, a singer/
songwriter who now works as a textile and fashion
designer, and her father is Gavin Rossdale, frontman for
the rock band Bush. Daisy's parents did not live together:
she was born when her mother was just 19, while Pearl
actually lived with Supergrass drummer Danny Goffey,
whom she married in 1995. Pearl was also a friend of
Kate Moss and a member of the notorious Primrose Hill
set, although by the time Daisy met Matt, the family
had long since settled into a quiet life in Hampshire,
where the wildness of yesteryear was a thing of the
past. That said, Daisy did not actually accompany them:
she stayed with her grandparents in London to complete
her schooling.

'I think I just needed to have a go at rebelling,' was how

Daisy described her decision to stay on at school, study hard and gain nine excellent GCSEs. 'The minute she [Pearl] got out of London I was happy she had got away but it just wasn't for me. She is a great mum and a great role model for me. The benefit of having a mum so young is that I get to live so much of my life with her. It makes me want to have children when I am still young. I definitely want to have kids by the time I am 26.' Matt – take note!

Daisy's career kicked off when she was pretty young: she started modelling at the age of two, and by her mid-teens was taking part in various photo shoots. At 15 she was signed up by the Select modelling agency and started appearing in some of the glossiest magazines in the world, among them *Vogue*, *Tatler* and *Harper's Bazaar*. She also appeared on the catwalk for some of the world's most famous designers, among them Chanel, Burberry and Vivienne Westwood. Her career, to put it mildly, was doing well.

She also started DJing and getting into music – much like Matt's previous girlfriend, in fact. However, her background was very unlike Matt's normal, middle-class oasis of stability. Pearl had been married before, to Bronner Lowe, and Daisy had grown up believing him to be her father. It was only when Daisy found out that neither Bronner nor Pearl had O-type blood that she demanded the truth and sought a paternity test via her lawyers, much to the reported angst of Gavin's wife Gwen Stefani. And so she found her real father. She was forced to grow up very fast.

In reality, unlike Matt, she had been in the full glare of publicity all her life. 'A lot of the stuff that gets written is just complete, mindless bullshit,' she said when she was just 16. 'If something bad is said about any of the people around me, then we all have a conversation about it [...] Most of the time it doesn't have an effect on my life. It's annoying when teachers say they've read things about me, and my head of year takes me aside and asks if I'm all right [...] But you've got to deal with it. There's no point going to cry in the toilet.' Perhaps not, but it was a lot for a young woman to take on board.

It was not difficult to see what Matt saw in Daisy. At almost exactly the moment that he came back on the dating scene again himself, Daisy took part in a very raunchy shot for Agent Provocateur, wearing nipple tassels and not a great deal else. Daisy herself was not available, however: she was dating Will Cameron. She was also based largely in New York. However, she came back to Britain frequently, and New York is not as far away as Rio de Janeiro. And so the seeds of romance were sown.

It was not, however, until April 2010, that it became public that the two were an item. The couple were seen at the Coachella music festival in Los Angeles all over each other: if the relationship had ever been secret, the secret was well and truly out. 'They couldn't get enough of each other and Matt didn't want to leave her side,' said one observer. 'Laughing and whispering into each other's ears, they didn't seem at all fazed by people watching them. They caught the Hot Chip set and were snogging each other's faces off to the song "Hand Me Down Your Love". Matt then bought her a flaxseed pizza. He told his mate she was a girl he could settle down with. Daisy says her stepdad Danny Goffey is a massive *Who* fan so hopefully they'll get on really well.'

Matt was sought after from other quarters as well. Women were now routinely throwing themselves at him, not least because he was clearly on his way to becoming an A-list star. 'His life is changing hugely all the time,' said a friend. 'Since the new *Doctor Who* series started on BBC1 last month, interest in him has gone through the roof. He used to be seen as a bit of a geek who wasn't exactly fighting off babes. Now he's got a hot girlfriend and other girls can't keep their hands off him. It's amazing to see how his life has changed.'

There was another potential obstacle: Daisy's mother Pearl. The two were extremely close, and Matt had yet to pass the Pearl test – although that was not always failsafe, as a previous boyfriend of Daisy, Mark Ronson, had found out. 'I want Mum to approve,' said Daisy. 'I can't be with them unless she approves of them … Yeah, she liked Mark too much and that freaked me out, so that's maybe why that ended. She had me so young and there is such a small gap between us that she always treated me as an equal rather than as a child. I grew up thinking I was a little adult, Mum's little mate.'

The duo were in the States for the American premiere of *Doctor Who*: it seemed to be going down just as well over there as it was in the UK, with Matt and Karen making a short, whistle-stop tour. And the stakes were huge. '*Doctor Who* has a cult following in the States thanks to David Tennant, but bosses are really hopeful that Matt and Karen can help to make the series even bigger,' said a BBC source. 'If the Doctor can work his magic, the pair will become worldwide stars.'

Matt was beginning to reap the rewards of his success in more than just his love life: he had signed a three-year deal with the BBC worth £600,000 to play the Doctor and had just bought his first property: a £775,000 converted church in Highgate, north London. 'It was a gamble to cast a relative unknown, but it's paid off spectacularly,' said a BBC insider. 'And just like the Doctor, Matt is a quirky guy and didn't want a run-of-the mill home, but something a bit different.'

But then a note of confusion struck. According to Daisy's mother Pearl, they were not an item at all – simply just good friends. 'Matt is a good friend,' she said. 'Daisy is just having fun. She's just finished a long-term relationship and she wants to concentrate on her modelling. Daisy would be silly to get tied down, I want her to do the opposite of what I did.' What Matt thought about that was not clear – but it was not long before the duo was looking pretty much like a couple again.

Matt was really on a roll now. The previous year, David Tennant had dropped a very big hint to the effect that he might be making a reappearance in the Tardis on the show's fiftieth anniversary in 2013, but added, apropos Matt, 'He's brilliant, which is annoying. There is no one who has worked with Matt in the UK who doesn't rave about him.' It was clear the rest of the country was beginning to agree. Matt made the 'Chart of Lust 2009' in the *Observer* magazine: 'The incoming *Doctor Who* is as fit as he is accomplished,' it pronounced. 'And he has well nice clothes, both in and out of character.'

Matt and Karen were out on the promotional trail throughout much of the first half of 2010; as they were doing so, Doctor Who was voted the greatest screen 'doctor' of all time. 'I think notions of sci-fi being geeky are outdated,' said Dave Bradley, editor of *SFX* magazine. 'Sci-fi in general, and *Doctor Who* in particular, are part of the mainstream now. *Doctor Who* has become the most popular non-soap drama on British TV, and words like Dalek are now in the dictionary. There's a whole generation of people who aren't afraid to openly love sci-fi, and I think *Doctor Who* has been part of that.'

Matt single-handedly kick-started a new fashion for tweed; the geography teacher look (which he admittedly excelled at) was all the rage. 'Originally I was going to have a black leather or a blue swashbuckling coat and possibly a hat too but, somewhere along the line, the idea got dropped,' Matt confided. 'I hope it's revived in time for series two.' But others thought it was high time that the Doctor was so well dressed: 'The whole thing of being a proper gent over the last few years has been very big,' said Daryoush Hal-Najafi, editor of vicestyle.com, a fashion website. 'He looks stylish. They've gone back to their roots with the mad professor thing, with the bow-tie.'

In fact, the possible addition of a coat was more than just a style decision. A lot of filming was done in the winter, and that tweed jacket, stylish as it was, was not enough to ward off the cold. 'It's been extremely cold shooting outdoor scenes for series one and I'm hoping the show's producers extend the Doctor's wardrobe for the next series – definitely to a coat and possibly a hat, as well!' he said in another interview. 'At one point, it looked as if he might wear a black leather coat – but, in the end – it was decided he would go without. It was a decision I was starting to regret when temperatures plummeted in December!'

More and more came out about how everyone had been preparing themselves. 'I wanted to feel like Doctor Who, understand where he'd come from,' mused Matt.

'So I wrote stories of the Doctor and Einstein in Egypt, which focused on their roles in the creation of the Pyramids. I had six months prep before we began filming so it gave me time to write quite a few stories.' Another detail emerged – the Daleks were shorter in this series. The programme-makers liked their sink plunger to be directly on a level with the Doctor's face, and at 5ft 10, Matt was three inches shorter than David Tennant. And so the Daleks shrank.

It had been very hard work. 'If you're ill, it's tough,' said Matt. 'I think your head would have to be falling off before you could take a day off.' As for the sonic screwdrivers – 'I've broken four of them,' said Matt. 'I like to have it about my person at all times, just twirling it around and flicking it. It's all part of the magic, isn't it?' Not always – Matt was stopped by security when trying to board a plane to Northern Ireland until he explained to the bemused security men who he was.

The series debuted on 3 April 2010 with 8.4 million viewers: Matt was deemed a triumph. In fact, so much was he a triumph, that another idea was put on the backburner: a *Doctor Who* film. This had actually been planned with David Tennant in mind, not Matt Smith, which set up a conflict of interest. 'There was a lot of excitement over the idea but now there's a general acceptance it isn't going to happen soon,' said a source. 'David's clearly in demand but there's also a feeling it'd be unfair on Matt to have a rival Doctor in cinemas.' And it was by no means certain which of them was now the more popular Doctor.

There was a certain amount of shock in April, shortly after the new series began, when a 1960s memo from the BBC bosses who had originally commissioned the show came to light. The Doctor, as imagined in 1966, was about to regenerate – and in the groovy Sixties take on the whole thing, was going to have a rather hallucinatory experience. 'It is as if he has had the LSD drug and instead of experiencing the kicks, he has the hell and dank horror which can be its effect,' the memo read. Not that there was anything of this about the clean-living Matt's take on the character: the Doctor had never been so fit, healthy and glad to be alive.

Karen decided to adopt the same healthy path. She was greatly embarrassed when pictures of her emerged looking very much the worse for wear after a night out on the tiles: Karen laughed it off. 'I think I am going to try and lay off falling out of nightclubs,' she said. 'It's not a good look!'

Karen, like Matt, was not going to complain. She was well aware of the opportunity that had been offered to both of them, and was as determined as he was to put it to good use. 'I'm embracing being recognised because it means people are interested in the show and that can only be a good thing,' she said in an interview after the show had started to air. 'My plan is to be really nice all the time. Steven has created this fantastic girl. She is a warrior. She will throw herself straight into the fray, probably stupidly sometimes. There have been a few of those big moments already and there are lots more to come.'

And then, of course, there was Matt – 'He is just a really creative soul,' said Karen. 'Matt has inspired me to keep trying new things. We have this crazy experience that we are sharing and have become good friends. We have had to prove ourselves but he is a brilliant Doctor.' Everyone else agreed.

Matt and Karen were beginning to make the news for very trivial reasons now. In April, there was havoc in the airlines industry, when planes were not able to travel to Europe, because of ash clouds created by an exploding Icelandic volcano. Matt and Amy were stranded in LA: this was duly reported.

Matt was earning praise for his geekiness, as opposed to his two predecessors' cool. 'There's a nice moment where the Doctor hangs from the strap on the ceiling and it breaks,' Steven Moffat said in April, talking about that week's episode, 'The Time Of Angels'. 'The very first time Matt did it, it was an accident – he wasn't supposed to do that; that's just typical Matt, breaking everything. He just tries to carry it off as a sort of Stan Laurel moment. It's extremely charming. Chris and David were quite cool, and while Matt certainly isn't short on cool, he has an amazing clumsiness.' He did indeed, which was what partly gave his turn as the Doctor such comic charm.

And the Matt Smith effect continued. It wasn't just sales of tweed jackets that were shooting up; so, too, were bow ties, by 94 per cent. Radley Bags were branching into tweed: they ordered a special cloth to be made at Harris Tweed's plant in Lewis.

Doctor Who was also attracting comment from some pretty unexpected quarters. Terry Pratchett, of all people, the famous author of the *Discworld* novels (and a direct inspiration for the episode 'The Beast Below') appeared to be lashing out at the show on surprising grounds: 'It is very, very entertaining,' he said in his role as guest editor of *SFX* magazine. 'I just wish that it was not classified as science fiction. *Who*'s science is pixel-thin, ludicrous. Only people who don't know what science fiction is say that *Doctor Who* is science fiction.' It was surprising criticism, and hotly disputed. This was the most popular science-fiction show on the box.

Stephen Fry was later going to be contributing to the debate, as well, and equally surprisingly, albeit on different grounds. But for now, he was full of nothing but praise: in the wake of 'The Vampires of Venice', he wrote on Twitter. 'Far and away Matt's Smith's best performance so far. When he's serious, grave and dignified and not being silly, he is simply superb.'

It was a funny experience watching what was

happening to Matt, for his friends and family as well as himself. Polly Stenham, the playwright who had caused such acclaim with *That Face*, was herself having to deal with the pressures of fame, but it was a breeze compared to Matt. 'Very occasionally, I get recognised, but it's not fame, which is something I'd hate anyway,' she said. 'Matt is one of my best friends, so it's nothing compared to the absolute insane weirdness that he has. You can't cross the street with him now without it being just crazy.' But he was coping: he knew just how lucky he was.

As the new series continued to garner praise, Stephen Fry stuck his oar in again, but this time in a very different way. Delivering the BAFTA Annual Television Lecture in London, Fry criticized the 'infantilism' of British television, singling out *Doctor Who*. The programmes were, 'like a chicken nugget. Every now and again we all like it … But if you are an adult you want something surprising, savoury, sharp, unusual, cosmopolitan, alien, challenging, complex, ambiguous, possibly even slightly disturbing and wrong. You want to try those things, because that's what being adult means.'

It was a surprising attack, not least because it had been no time at all since he'd been praising Matt on Twitter. Those with long memories recalled that Fry had penned an episode of *Doctor Who* in 2006 that had never actually been filmed; Steven Moffat, meanwhile, was not going to take this lying down. 'It was designed as a family programme,' he said. 'It's the junction between children's programmes and adults' programmes. It's the one everybody sits and watches. So it is for adults, it is for children, it's a rather brilliant idea – why don't we make a television programme that everybody wants to watch, very, very specifically? [But] I love Stephen and Stephen loves *Doctor Who.*'

Matt was coping admirably with the attention and the pressures that were coming his way, but even he felt the weight of the burden he was carrying upon those slim shoulders. Now that it was all in the can, he confessed to a severe bout of nerves in the first week of filming: 'I rang my dad, and said, 'I am in trouble,' he revealed. But to the great relief of many Who fans, his father talked him round.

It wasn't only Matt, however, who was feeling the pressure. His on-off relationship with Daisy was back on again, but it was reported that she was getting pretty fed up with the way women acted around her man. 'Daisy gets really jealous about all the female attention Matt gets,' said one source close to the couple. 'Girls literally throw themselves at him and it seriously winds her up. Daisy pulled the plug on their relationship after three months as she was sick of Matt hanging out in Camden with female fans. He would spend nights in The Hawley Arms surrounded by groupies and pretty girl friends. Daisy couldn't control her jealousy so finished with him. She's banned Matt from hanging around with a girl friend called Anastacia who's in a band and she's asked him to sever ties with his sexy Brazilian ex-girlfriend Mayana Moura. Matt was thinking about visiting Rio to see her but he won't be now, unless he's a fool.'

Indeed, Matt seemed to be loving every minute of his new status. 'Matt loves his new bachelor pad and has told mates he won't be inviting Daisy to move in any time soon as he wants some man time to do whatever he wants,' said a friend.

But there were benefits to his new life, too. Matt played opposite Alison Hammond on ITV's *This Morning* in a table soccer match: he won, and received a signed Blackburn Rovers strip. For a man as football mad as Matt that was quite something: 'Thank you so much, and thank you Blackburn Rovers,' he said, clearly moved. 'It's the best.'

And he got to do other things that the Doctor would clearly have considered to be cool. At Glastonbury, Orbital performed on the Other Stage, and got Matt Smith to join in for their version of the *Doctor Who* theme song, something that sent the crowds mad. Matt looked as if he was pretty happy, too. Indeed – everyone was a winner. And some were on the verge of becoming very rich indeed.

CHAPTER 14
WHO'S IN THE MONEY?

Now that Matt had been firmly established as the Eleventh Doctor, a lot of people were very satisfied, because quite apart from all the kudos and the artistic achievement, it looked as if a lot of people were going to get very rich. Matt's own £600,000 contract was very generous by most people's standards, of course, and he was doing pretty well for a man still in his twenties, but it was hardly in the mega-million league that a bona fide Hollywood star could expect. However, industry experts pointed out that he would earn a lot more by way of 'residuals' – namely, the merchandise that bore his face. Some people believed that if he played his cards right, a small fortune could be heading his way – with the brand as a whole worth as much as £100 million.

The fact that he was going down so well in the United States helped. 'Matt will help broaden the show's appeal away from sci-fi geeks and little kids and attract more girl fans,' said a source at the BBC. 'At present, the show is seen only on BBC America but we're hopeful that it will be picked up by one of the major networks. We are confident the *Doctor Who* brand can become a £100 million business within the next few years.'

Doctor Who merchandise was, it should be said, nothing new. It dated right back to the very beginning of the series: in 1964 there was a board game called Dodge the Daleks, and the following year there were another three, called The Dalek Oracle, Dalek Shooting Game and Daleks: The Great Escape. Since then there had been board games, card games, role-playing games, miniature war games, pinball and computer games. There had been picture cards, action figures, money banks, key rings, Tardis-shaped clocks, Sonic Screwdriver pens, a Dalek USB Flash Memory Stick and even stamps. Then there were *Doctor Who* books, magazines and comic books. There were *Doctor Who* medals made by the Royal Mint. There was everything you could possibly want.

Some *Doctor Who* memorabilia had even become collectable. Action figures from the 1970s could net a great deal: Tom Baker figures started at about $75, but rare figures could go for a great deal more. In May 2006, a Denys Fisher Dalek with its box sold for $1150. Bonhams once held a sale of *Doctor Who* memorabilia: it raised £250,000. It was possible to buy life size Daleks from about £1,895, while older models could go for as much as £36,000. A Cyberman could fetch £9,600. The stakes were high.

The last David Tennant series did spectacularly well. According to BBC Worldwide, selling to over 50 territories, it sold more than 3.3 million DVDs, more than seven million action figures and about 300,000 books in 2009 alone. And that's not counting Dalek masks, Cybermen masks, pencil cases and folders, thought to be worth about another £10 million.

Steven Moffat had no intention of exploiting the 'brand' per se, for purely marketing purposes, although he did acknowledge it was there. 'To me, a "brand" sounds evil, reminiscent of men in tall hats running factories and beating small children, but you have to be across it,' he said. 'All those things should be joyous – those toys should be terrific – because the active creative engagement of children with *Doctor Who* is unlike any other show that they watch. When *Doctor Who* is over, they get up, invent their own monster, their own planet, their own Doctor and play. I know because my son recently designed a new Tardis control room. If anyone said to me "invent a new monster so we can sell more toys", I'd kick them out of my office.'

In fact, a whole industry had built up around the series. 'Despite the recession we've gone from strength to strength,' said Alexandra Looseley-Saul, who runs The Who Shop in East London. 'In hard times people escape to nostalgia and fantasy. One of our hottest items is a replica of David Tennant's brown trench coat which we sell for £350.'

Then there was Ian Clarke, who made *Doctor Who* memorabilia to order, for merchandising company The Planet Earth, including Daleks and Tardises. 'They are the ultimate toy – and people find them impressive,' he said. 'They are very popular with celebrities. Harry Hill and Liam from The Prodigy both bought one. One couple bought a Tardis as a changing room for their swimming pool and someone else bought another one to use as a shower room.'

And so, with Matt as the new Doctor, the new merchandising machine went into action. After the series began in 2010, the first three episodes were released on DVD, selling more than 13,000 in the first week. In April, three hardback *Doctor Who* novels were published: all made it into the Top 10. 'Asda took them as Book of the Month for teens, which has never been done before, and was such a success they're planning the same for the next release,' said a source at the BBC.

Meanwhile, *Doctor Who Adventures* magazine had relaunched, with a new website; there was a console video game by Nintendo in the offing; Character Options, which licensed the toys, was producing a new set of figures; and a new Sonic Screwdriver had hit the market.

There were plans for a *Doctor Who* Arena tour in the autumn, interactive PC and Mac games and a range of Penguin books. 'If *Doctor Who* were sold tomorrow, it would be worth about £100 million and as the earnings continue to grow, Matt will make more and more money,' said a source.

When David Tennant was the Doctor, more than 20 types of action figures based on him went up for sale. Matt could expect something similar, and it was also a gauge of his popularity to see how fast the shops were selling out. And they were: the first model, still wearing David Tennant's torn clothing rather than the tweed jacket and bow tie he would make his own, sold out almost immediately. Matt's bemused mother Lynne was impressed. 'The likeness is incredible,' she said. 'It's amazing, I think it's a really good model of him. And he's my son, so I've obviously looked at it really closely. It was fabulous to see his first model, it was really exciting for us all.' The official sale price was £8.99 but the models were already trading on eBay for £20 to £30.

The interest just could not be overestimated. There was a *Doctor Who* Collectors Wiki, a database of Doctor Who merchandise to which anyone can contribute, untold numbers of fan sites and a seemingly insatiable appetite for *Doctor Who* products from all over the world.

Matters had now also got to a state where Matt needed an assistant of his own. Enter Lynne, who decided to give up work to help run the affairs of her increasingly famous son. 'With all the *Doctor Who* stuff, Matt really needed somebody to run his fan club, so I thought what better than to keep it in the family because nobody else is going to do it like me,' she said. 'I think everybody who writes in should get an autograph, because he needs his fans. And already, we've had loads of stuff coming in. From the day he was first announced as the new Doctor, people have been writing to him from all over the world. We've had stuff come from Australia where somebody sent him a T-shirt with a Matt Smith logo on it, and he's had hundreds of Christmas cards, birthday cards, all sorts of things.' And it was bound to go on in leaps and bounds from there.

And so yet another industry began to grow up: that around Matt himself. The predictions that he might end up as the wealthiest Doctor boded well for his future, whatever turn his actual career took, for in one sense, at least, he was set up for life. Matt was now an established, property-owning actor, with a great career in front of him and, if he played his cards right, a considerable amount of money in the bank. He was being given that which actors value above all else – choice. Matt was already well on the way to being able to pick and choose his roles, with little to hold him back from joining the ranks of the greats. All he needed now was sound judgement – and not to lose his nerve.

CHAPTER 15

BACK TO THE FUTURE

Although all sorts of glory beckoned Matt at such a very young age, there was still one danger: that the role of Doctor Who would overshadow anything else he would ever do in his career. The very fact he was so young was an element in his favour, because it gave him plenty of time to seek out other projects, but nonetheless, it was something he had to be aware of. Even Christopher Eccleston, the shortest-ever serving Doctor, could not get away from the role: just after Matt's first series ended, Eccleston featured on a one-off film about John Lennon, in the title role. Even then, he was spoken of as a past Who. And Matt had certainly made an impact in the role. He was up for Best Actor at the TV Choice Awards, while Karen was up for Best Actress and the show itself for Best Family Drama. It was the first time the Doctor and his assistant had made the same shortlist.

Matt, of course, was well aware that there were some hard choices to make somewhere along the line. A similarly iconic role to the Doctor was that of James Bond, which would be up for grabs at some point in the future, but he saw himself as the bad guy in that one, not the good. 'I don't think I'm handsome enough,' he said of the James Bond role. 'I think I'd make a quite good young Bond villain. It would be kind of nice though to be the actor who's done both. I've never got away with being the handsome leading man. I suppose I'm the peculiar, odd lead. Which may work in my favour.'

That certainly applied to his role as the Doctor: a sort of but not quite romantic hero. 'The Doctor's a bit bumbly, isn't he? He doesn't really know what to do with women,' he said. 'People ask me "Who do you think your Doctor is?" and I'm reluctant to think of it in those terms, because it's still a work in progress. Steven Moffat, who's just the most brilliant writer, told me when I first met him that the interesting thing, the defining thing, about the Doctor is that he never quite knows what's going to come out of his mouth in any given situation. His thoughts just combust spontaneously. I've tried to harness that brain-to-mouth rapidity. I mean, you could think about it forever, but how do you play the most charismatic man in the universe? It's a real challenge. If you play him consciously charismatic, he instantly loses the charisma.

'Of course, really charismatic people don't have to do a

thing. They just are. I'm still finding my way on that one, but I like to think it gives me something creative to play with. Hopefully we see him in the white heat of danger, flying by the seat of his pants. He's also funny and he has great courage and this enormous intellect, but all the great Doctors have had that. As a character, he kind of belongs to everyone. Everyone has their own identity for him. Mine is probably different, but I've become a real fan. I know it sounds very vain, but I do look forward to the ceremony of watching the show on a Saturday night.'

The James Bond connection was an intriguing one, however, and Matt had, coincidentally, signed up to work with an actress who was already associated with 007. Just before he got the part of Doctor Who, he signed up to star in a film called *Womb*, alongside the previous Bond girl Eva Green, a film, according to the producers that 'tells the story of a grieving widow, played by Green, who decides to clone her late husband,' It was a story about the efforts to overcome death by genetic manipulation.

The script was written by Benedek Fliegauf. According to the production team, 'it deals with the moral and ethical issues surrounding human cloning, but in a sensitive and all too believable story. It inexorably draws us in to the world of the characters, so that we can identify on an intimate personal level with the human dilemmas that confront them. It should be a profoundly moving film that will deeply effect audiences, and stir debate about this issue.'

In fact Matt's role in *Womb* could not have been more different from that of Doctor Who. A German production, it was a story about a young woman, played by Eva, who returned to her grandfather's home on the North Sea of Germany, and who is reunited with her childhood sweetheart, only to see him die in a car accident. She resorts to cloning to bring him back to life. She played Rebecca and Matt was Thomas.

'We've spent four years developing this project,' said Roman Paul, one of the film's producers. 'What I liked about Benedek's previous films is that they're so unique and have an almost hypnotic quality. His films have to be experienced in their entirety. For example, you cannot take the acting or the production design on their own, but have to see everything together as a whole.'

The decision to cast Matt in the role came about precisely because he didn't look like James Bond. 'Matt is quite extraordinary because he's an actor who works from the gut rather than the brain,' said Fliegauf. 'He's really connected with real life somehow, whereas Eva looks one time like Disney's Snow White and then like an actress from a Murnau [influential director of the silent era] film. She has no connection with the real world whereas Matt's feet are firmly on the ground. I didn't want to choose the classical beauty for the male lead because then it would have been rather weird if she made the decision to clone him because of the physical aspect. It's more about the soul.'

The film, which took just over a month to make, was set around Hallig Langeness, Sylt and St Peter-Ording in northern Germany. 'It took a while to find the locations because the setting for the film is not specific. It's somewhere in the North by the sea,' said Paul. '*Womb* is a modern fairytale in the style of, say, [nineteenth-century writer] ETA Hoffmann — it's set in our world but given a fictional twist.'

Filming was a mixed experience for Matt. On the one hand Eva was widely held to be one of the most beautiful women in the world; on the other the whole experience had been downright painful. 'We were on the north German coast and the script called for me to run into the Baltic without any clothes on,' he related. 'In the middle of bloody winter, mind. Oh my God, how freezing was that? It was the coldest I'd ever been and, of course, it just so happened to be my first scene with Eva. I had to get out of the water and do the whole thing in front of her stark bollock naked. That's not a good lot for any man, let me tell you.'

In fact he needed the attention of a doctor. 'They said I could use a double, but I'd worked myself up to do it so I went into the sea three times,' he said. 'The next shot we did, we were running along the beach and I was so frozen I couldn't move. I just hit the deck.'

A very different role was as Christopher, in *Christopher and His Kind*, about the writer Christopher Isherwood. It was a film written by Kevin Elyot for the BBC and reunited Matt with his *That Face* co-star Lindsay Duncan, again playing his mother, again a domineering and suffocating character – but this time one he managed to escape. Christopher leaves Britain for Berlin in the 1930s, which was indeed a seminal point in Isherwood's career, for it was there that he wrote the Berlin stories that were eventually going to inspire the musical and film *Cabaret*. Other characters in the drama were Jean Ross (Imogen Poots), an aspiring actress who was to be the inspiration for Sally Bowles in *Cabaret*, Gerald Hamilton (Toby Jones), a funny little man later immortalised in *Mr Norris Changes Trains*, the poet W.H. Auden (Pip Carter) and Heinz (Douglas Booth), a street cleaner with whom Christopher falls in love. For Isherwood was, of course, a gay man – a world removed from the Doctor, and indeed, from the character in *Womb*. Matt was clearly picking roles as diverse as he could in order to avoid the typecasting pitfalls that lay ahead.

There was, inevitably, a certain amount of controversy surrounding it all. The film was shot in Belfast, rather than Berlin, and eyebrows were raised when the Nazi flag was hung in the courtyard of Belfast city hall. Then there was to be a gay snog with Douglas Booth (who had also played the title role in a film about Boy George), which would have pleased Russell T Davies, if nothing else, since he had brought in the slightly bisexual but probably more gay than anything else, Captain Jack Harkness, the time traveller played by John Barrowman in both *Doctor Who* and the spin-off series *Torchwood*.

Matt certainly seemed to be coping with his new found fame. There were no signs of ego: he was maintaining a level-headed attitude to it all. 'Being recognised in the streets is a new experience for me, but it's certainly not a bad experience,' he said. 'I'm guessing the trick with being in the eye of the media is to ignore the bad publicity – and perhaps even the things that are good – because, artistically, each is as dangerous as the other.'

He had also brought innovation to the role, not least because, in 'The Lodger', there had appeared to be a nude scene, a first for the Doctor. Matt was pictured in the shower, his modesty protected by a shower curtain, before flinging himself out of the bathroom, grabbing a towel en route. Delighted fans claimed that they had seen parts of the Doctor never pictured on the small screen before; the BBC was adamant, however, that nothing unseemly had taken place. Matt was wearing some form of cover-up, it was said. Still, it was undoubtedly taking the Doctor into areas he had never ventured into before. Could there ultimately be romance on the cards? It had been hinted at enough in this series, but everyone was agreed that there was too much of a danger of spoiling the dramatic tension. And anyway, Amy had finally got married. She and the Doctor looked destined to remain just good friends.

So what next? Matt was in an unusual position, in that he had the world at his feet while he was still a very young man and yet still had to avoid becoming known for one role alone. 'It's an infinite narrative and there are infinite sides of the character that you can explore,' said Matt of his role as the Doctor, but the fact is that the Doctor is still the Doctor. No one actor has ever proven to be greater than the part.

But then none has been as young as Matt Smith. Could the role of James Bond beckon? Despite Matt's own reservations, there would certainly be a sort of resonance to one actor playing the two great iconic roles in British popular culture. Roles in Shakespeare are almost certainly his for the asking (David Tennant played Hamlet to great acclaim and it would be very interesting to see Matt's version, too). On top of that, he looks increasingly likely to become a heartthrob. Matt might not have been classically handsome, but his energy and excitement made him a very attractive proposition. And he certainly wasn't short of female fans.

But for the next few years, at least, Matt will inhabit the Tardis, with more specials and another series to come, and with Karen also looking set to stay. Soprano

Katherine Jenkins and legendary actor Michael Gambon are set to star in this year's Christmas special of *Doctor Who*, which according to Steven Moffat is set to be 'the most Christmassy Christmas special' since the cult TV series returned to the screens back in 2005.

The question 'Matt Who?' has long been answered. The only one remaining is this: Who could possibly take over the role from Matt now?